Their Mnew

Them Personal Reminiscences of the Kings and Queens of Europe

Xavier Paoli

Alpha Editions

This edition published in 2023

ISBN : 9789357943024

Design and Setting By
Alpha Editions
www.alphaedis.com
Email - info@alphaedis.com

As per information held with us this book is in Public Domain.
This book is a reproduction of an important historical work. Alpha Editions uses the best technology to reproduce historical work in the same manner it was first published to preserve its original nature. Any marks or number seen are left intentionally to preserve its true form.

Contents

INTRODUCTION .... - 1 -
I .... - 8 -
II .... - 27 -
III .... - 47 -
IV .... - 72 -
V .... - 90 -
VI .... - 107 -
VII .... - 122 -
VIII .... - 137 -
IX .... - 157 -
X .... - 172 -
FOOTNOTES: .... - 183 -

INTRODUCTION

M. XAVIER PAOLI

THE "CHAMBERLAIN" OF THE FRENCH REPUBLIC AND THE FRIEND OF SOVEREIGNS

It was in 1903, and the King of England was making his first official journey in France since succeeding Queen Victoria on the throne of Great Britain. In the court of the British Embassy in Paris, where the sovereign had taken up his residence, a group of journalists, pencil and notebook in hand, was crowding importunate, full of questions, around a vivacious little gentleman, very precisely dressed in black, wearing the red rosette of the Legion of Honour in the buttonhole of his silk-faced frock coat. An impressive silk hat, slightly tipped, sheltered a head of abundant wavy white hair, strikingly in contrast with the man's still youthful appearance; at the utmost he seemed to be hardly fifty years old.

His aristocratic bearing might have been that of a diplomat of the Empire or a Tuscan aristocrat. The sensitive features of his finely oval face—the straight, delicately formed nose, the piercing eyes, now bright with shrewd humour, now soft with gentle sympathy—all spoke the judicial mind, the penetrating observation, which could scrutinise the most secret thoughts, recognise the slightest shades of feeling.

Calmly, manfully, smilingly, with courtesy, the little gentleman sustained the assault of the reporters and warded off their indiscreet curiosity.

"What did the King say to M. Loubet?"

"Gentlemen, the King has told me none of his secrets."

"Did he not come for the purpose of completing a treaty of military alliance with us, and is he not to have this evening an important interview with the Minister of Foreign Affairs?"

"His Majesty had a very comfortable journey, is in the best of spirits, and appears to be delighted to be in Paris."

"But—"

"His Majesty brought with him his little griffon dog, and immediately on arriving he asked for port wine and sandwiches."

"I beg—"

"I may even say that the King will go to hear Sarah Bernhardt this evening, and that at the present moment he is busy with his secretary looking over the voluminous mail which has just arrived from London. In fact—"

"Pardon me—is it true that yesterday you arrested some suspected anarchists?"

"Anarchists? What are they?" And with these words the little gentleman still smiling turned away, to the discomfiture of the journalists, while certain English and French officers who, full of excitement, were crossing the great court, saluted him with courteous deference.

This little gentleman, whom I then saw for the first time, was M. Xavier Paoli.

When the time comes for writing the history of the Third French Republic—not its political history, which is already sufficiently well known, but the other, its picturesque, anecdotic, private history, that which must be sought behind the scenes of a government, and shows the little causes which often produced the great effects—when that history comes to be written, it is certain that a long chapter and perhaps the most interesting, will be devoted to M. Paoli.

He is, in fact, a unique and singular character, a personage "apart," extraordinarily attractive, somewhat disconcerting, but wonderfully interesting in the group of French functionaries who have rendered real and precious service to their country. His official title was until very recently, and had been for twenty-five years, that of Special Commissioner of Railways for the Ministry of the Interior. This title, somewhat commonplace, is in itself intentionally obscure, tells nothing of the man or his office. The old proverb says: "The habit does not make the monk," and it may here be added that the title does not always designate the function. Attached to the political police, but in no respect appearing like a policeman, a sort of Sherlock Holmes, but a very high and particular ideal of Sherlock Holmes until now unknown, M. Paoli's three-fold and delicate mission was to watch over the foreign sovereigns and princes who for the past twenty-five years had been coming to France incognito, to facilitate their relations with the government, and on the whole, to quote M. Paoli's own words "to make their stay among us as pleasant as possible." "The guardian of Kings," as the King of Greece one day called him, was at the same time a keen diplomat. He, in fact, personified and filled an office which, notwithstanding its paradoxical aspect, proved to be of incontestible utility: he was the Grand Chamberlain of the Republic, accredited to its imperial and royal guests.

How was he brought to take up this important and difficult duty? How did he come to have all the necessary qualities to perform it, as he did,

with equally remarkable facility, ease and tact? Psychology makes answer that motives must be sought in the origin, the early experience and subsequent career of the personality with whom we are concerned.

Like the great Napoleon, for whom he has always felt a touching adoration, M. Paoli is a Corsican. He was born in 1835 at La Porta, a picturesque little town perched like an eagle's nest on the crest of a hill on the eastern slope of the island, overlooking the sea, with the Island of Elba and the coast of Tuscany in the distance. His ancestor was that celebrated and fiery General Paoli, who at the close of the previous century stirred up a patriotic agitation in Corsica; on his mother's side he was a descendant of Marshal Sebastiani, who was ambassador and minister of Foreign Affairs in the reign of Louis Philippe. From his earliest youth, Xavier Paoli, like all Corsicans was passionately interested in politics. In 1859 a decree of the Emperor Napoleon III, who greatly esteemed this honourable and popular family, nominated young Paoli mayor of La Porta. According to custom the young official went to Ajaccio to pay his respects to the Prefect. This high functionary, on perceiving him, could not conceal his surprise.

"I am much pleased to make your acquaintance, young man," he said, "but I had supposed that your father would come himself."

"The trouble is that my father has been dead for several years."

"What! He has not just now been nominated mayor of La Porta?"

"No, Mr. Prefect, it was I."

He was only twenty-five years old.

Two years later, being elected Councillor General of his canton, he united the two functions, giving to his fellow citizens an example of precocious administrative ability and a keen appreciation of the interests of his constituents. Local politics, however, "does not feed its men" as the proverb says, especially when like M. Paoli, the politician is thoroughly disinterested. The Paoli family had long been engaged in the oil trade, but the business which once brought in a comfortable livelihood had been declining, having been carried on with less perseverance and attention than formerly. Young Paoli perceived that he must not count upon the family business to make his fortune; in fact, politics were swallowing up his modest revenue. He, therefore, resolved to alter his plan of life, to leave the island where he had achieved a precocious popularity, where he was esteemed and beloved.

His friends in Paris proposed to obtain for him an under-prefecture, but he preferred a simple post of Police Magistrate at 1800 francs, to the great scandal of his family, who considered him to have lowered himself on entering the police service.

"Let me alone," replied M. Paoli, "I feel that my future is at stake, and that I shall be safer in being inconspicuous."

And, in fact, when, four years later, the Empire fell, it was due to the modesty of M. Paoli's position that he was not involved in the fall. At the time he was police commissary in the railway station at Modena on the Italian frontier, and he had the tact to make himself so useful to the new Prefect that although he by no means paid court to the new government, like so many others, the latter was glad to confirm him in his functions. The Modena station was an important outpost of observation and inspection on the great European highway, princes incognito, statesmen on their travels, Italian anarchists leaving their country on some mysterious mission—all passed that way. Not one of them escaped M. Paoli's vigilant eye. This humble position afforded him the opportunity to show his great qualifications of perspicacity and tact. He was sent to Nice, and other cosmopolitan centres, where all classes and peoples meet and mingle; before long he was called to Paris. It was at this juncture, and thanks to Queen Victoria, that his mission as "Guardian of Kings" became clear.

The French Republic was at that time by no means "persona grata" at foreign courts. The daughter of the Commune of 1871, her cap still vaguely besmirched, her acts problematical, they were all afraid of her, hardly daring to receive or to visit her. And yet some line of conduct must be adopted: it was not possible always to keep under ban the lovely land of France.

A little King of no importance—I think it was the King of Wurtemburg—was the first to risk himself among us. He was M. Paoli's first client.

When at last the Queen of England, upon the advice of her physicians, decided to exchange the chill banks of the Thames for the sunny gardens of the Côte d'Azur, it was to M. Paoli that the government of the Republic intrusted the duty of doing the honours of the French territory and assuring her safety during her sojourn among us. He acquitted himself of this delicate task with such success as immediately gained the confidence of the venerable Queen to such an extent that she desired her ambassador to write to the French Minister of Foreign Affairs that thenceforth she wished that no other functionary than M. Paoli should watch over her during her visits to France. Each year, therefore, she found him faithful to his charge, awaiting her arrival either at Cherbourg or Calais.

From this time, M. Paoli became the indispensable personage for all the sovereigns and princes who undertook to visit our country, and therefore indispensable to the Republican government, who found in M. Paoli a perfect intermediary between itself and them. During twenty-five years he successively escorted to our watering places and seashore resorts fifteen

emperors or kings, half a dozen empresses and queens, and countless numbers of princes of the blood, grand dukes and other princely globe trotters. He was admitted to their confidences, understood their impressions. To most of them, who continually saw our ministers appear and disappear, and who each time they came received the homage of new personages, M. Paoli personified the Republic which, with whatever petty quarrels and changes of officials, was always calm and smiling to its guests in the drawing-room. France, indeed, profited by the precious friendship which M. Paoli won for himself. "He is a model functionary, he has made the Republic beloved by Kings," exclaimed M. Félix Faure one day in my presence. And I remember another striking reflection of the regretted President.

As he came out of the hotel of the Empress of Austria where he had been visiting at Cap Martin, some one asked him what had been the subject of his interview with the sovereign.

"The Empress, gentlemen, spoke of nothing except of M. Paoli, whose courtesy and tact she praised without reserve."

What tribute could have been more flattering, indeed, than the invitation which he received from Queen Victoria to be present at her jubilee, and to accept the hospitality of Buckingham Palace? And after her death the royal family begged him to be present at her obsequies, and during all the sad solemnities treated him as a faithful and devoted friend.

And finally, what finer recognition of the "Protector of Sovereigns" than the remark of the King of England—then the Prince of Wales—when in the railway station of Brussels he was fired upon by the young anarchist Sipido—"If Paoli had been here," he said, "the rascal would have been arrested before he could use his weapon."

In fact, M. Paoli was always able to shield his clients from painful surprises and dramatic dangers. His art was always to appear ignorant of the fact that there were anarchists in the world, while at the same time keeping them constantly under the strictest watch. I believe that he was popular even among them, and that their esteem for this just and good man was so great that they would not, for anything in the world, have caused him—annoyance!

It is a curious fact that he never carried a weapon. The King of Siam was greatly disconcerted when he learned that M. Paoli had been charged to protect him during his visit to France in 1896.

"But where are your pistols and your poniards?" he would ask him every few minutes.

M. Paoli appears to cherish no vanity on account of the august interest with which he has been honoured, and the important part which during twenty-five years he has performed with as much intelligence as precision. He is still the affable and simple man which he always was. He may be the most decorated functionary in France—he possesses forty-two foreign decorations—but these seem to make him neither prouder nor happier. His only joy is to live quietly in his retreat, among his memories. His very modest apartment is a museum such as has no equal, harbouring all the sovereigns of yesterday and of to-day. Alphonso XIII and his young wife are in company with the royal pair of Italy, the Emperor of Russia seems to be conversing with the Emperor of Austria, the Queen of Saxony receives the salutation of the King of the Bulgarians, while listening to the poems which the Queen of Roumania appears to be reciting to her. The aged King Christian is smiling upon his innumerable grandchildren, the Prince of Wales is talking with his son, the Shah of Persia gazes upon the Bey of Tunis; and dominating all these crowned heads, the good Queen Victoria smiling from her golden frame, looks happily around upon all her family. To these photographs, each with its precious autograph, are added most touching testimonials of affection and esteem, letters entirely written by sovereign hands, jewels of inestimable price, the gifts of august clients. M. Paoli is in fact the only Frenchman who can at one time wear a cravat pin given by the Emperor of Austria, a watch offered by the King of Greece, a chain presented by Queen Victoria, a cane from the King of Sweden, a cigarette holder from the Emperor of Russia, a match box from the King of England, and—I cease, for the list would be interminable.

As may easily be perceived, the "Guardian of Kings" has often been asked to write his memoirs. One cannot have been intimate with sovereigns for twenty-five years and not have a whole book—many volumes, indeed—of impressions and memories in the brain. But precisely because he has been the travelling companion of illustrious guests of the nation, he has believed himself bound to absolute silence and a perhaps excessive discretion.

Happily, arguments have at last prevailed over these exaggerated scruples. M. Paoli has come to perceive that by relating his personal recollections, he would be making a useful contribution to the history of our time, correcting many errors which have slipped voluntarily or involuntarily into accounts of certain contemporary sovereigns.

M. Paoli has therefore yielded to persuasion, and has committed to writing the story of his many journeys in the company of Kings, reviving his memories of former days. I have been happy in collaborating with this interesting and charming man, and I hope that our readers may enjoy as happy hours in reading these memories as I myself have enjoyed in hearing them related to me.

RENE LARA.

I

THE EMPEROR AND EMPRESS OF AUSTRIA

1.

The infinitely fascinating and melancholy image of the Empress Elizabeth of Austria represents a special type among all the royal and imperial majesties to whose persons I have been attached during their different stays in France; and this both on account of her life, which was one long romance, and of her death, which was a tragedy.

Hers was a strong, sad soul; and she disappeared suddenly, as in a dream of terror. She hovers round my memory crowned with the halo of unhappiness.

The first time that I saw her was at Geneva; and I cannot recall this detail without emotion, for it was at Geneva that she was to die under the assassin's dagger. At the end of August, 1895, the Government received notice from the French Embassy in Vienna that the Empress was about to visit Aix-les-Bains in Savoy. She was to travel from her palace of Miramar through Italy and Switzerland; and, as usual, I received my formal letter of appointment from the Ministry of the Interior, instructing me to go and meet the Empress at the International railway-station at Geneva.

I confess that, when I stepped into the train, I experienced a keen sense of curiosity at the thought that I was soon to find myself in the presence of the lady who was already surrounded by an atmosphere of legend and who was known as "the wandering empress."

I had been told numerous more or less veracious stories of her restless and romantic life; I had heard that she talked little, that she smiled but rarely and that she always seemed to be pursuing a distant dream.

My first impression, however, when I saw her alighting from her carriage on the Geneva platform, was very different from that which I was prepared to receive. The Empress, at that time, was fifty-eight years of age. She looked like a girl, she had the figure of a girl, with a girl's lightness and grace of movement.

Tall and slender, with a touch of stiffness in her bearing, she had a rather fresh-coloured face, deep, dark and extraordinarily bright eyes and a wealth of chestnut hair. I realised later that she owed her vivacious colouring to the long walks which she was in the constant habit of taking. She wore a smartly-cut black tailor-made dress, which accentuated her slimness. The beauty of her figure was a matter of which she was frankly vain; she weighed herself every day.

I was also struck by the smallness of her hands, the musical intonation of her voice and the purity with which she expressed herself in French, although she pronounced it with a slightly guttural accent.

One disappointment, however, awaited me; my reception was icy cold. In spite of the experience which I had acquired during the exercise of my special functions, it left me none the less disconcerted. My feeling of discomfort was still further increased when, on reaching Aix-les-Bains, General Berzeviczy, whom I had asked for an interview in order to arrange for the organisation of my department, answered drily:

"We sha'n't want anybody."

These four words, beyond a doubt, constituted a formal dismissal, an invitation, both plain and succinct, to take the first train back to Paris. My position became one of singular embarrassment. Invested with a confidential mission, I was beginning by inspiring distrust precisely in those to whom this mission was addressed; charged to watch and remove "suspects," I myself appeared to be the most suspected of all!

Nevertheless, I resolved that I would not be denied. I organised my service without the knowledge of our guests. Every morning, I returned to see General Berzeviczy. Avoiding any allusion to the real object of my visit, I did my best to overcome his coldness. The general was a very kind man at heart and a charming talker. I therefore told him the gossip of the day, the news from Paris, the tittle-tattle of Aix. I advised excursions, pointed out the curiosities worth seeing, conscientiously fulfilled my part as a Baedeker, and, when I carelessly questioned the general concerning the Empress's intentions as to the employment of her day, he forgot himself to the extent of telling me. This was all that I wanted to know.

In a week's time we were the best of friends. The Empress had condescended to appreciate my frankness in daily covering the table with newspapers and reviews. She gradually became accustomed to seeing me appear just in time to forestall her wishes. The game was won; and, when, later, curious to know the cause of what appeared to me to have been a misunderstanding, I asked General Berzeviczy to explain the reason of his disconcerting reception, he replied:

"It was simply because, when we go abroad, they generally send us officials who, under the pretext of protecting us, terrorise us. They appear to us like Banquo's ghost, with doleful faces and shifting eyes; they see assassins everywhere; they poison and embitter our holidays. That is why you appeared so suspicious to us at first."

"And now?"

"Now," he answered with a smile, "the experiment has been made. You have fortunately broken with an ugly tradition. In your case, we forget the official, and remember only the friend."

2.

In the course of the three visits which the Empress Elizabeth paid to France between 1895 and 1898, I had every opportunity of studying, in the intimacy of its daily life, that little wandering court swayed by the melancholy and fascinating figure of its sovereign. She led an active and solitary existence. Rising, winter and summer, at five o'clock, she began by taking a warm bath in distilled water, followed by electric massage, after which, even though it were still dark, she would go out into the air.

Clad in a black serge gown, ultra-simple in character, she walked at a smart pace along the paths of the garden, or, if it were raining, perambulated the long passages which run out of the halls or "lounges" of most hotels. Sometimes she would venture on the roads and look for a fine point of view—by preference, the top of a rock—from which she loved to watch the sunrise.

She returned at seven o'clock and breakfasted lightly on a cup of tea with a single biscuit. She then disappeared into her apartments and devoted two hours to her toilet.

Her second meal was taken at eleven and consisted of a cup of clear soup, an egg and one or two glasses of meat-juice, extracted every morning out of several pounds of fillet of beef by means of a special apparatus which accompanied her on her travels. She also tasted a light dish or two, with a preference for sweets. Immediately after lunch, she went out again, accompanied, this time, by her Greek reader.

This Greek reader was a very important person. He formed one of the suite on every journey. Selected from among the young scholars of the University of Athens, and often appointed by the Greek Government, he was changed year by year. I, for my part, have known three different readers. Their duties consisted in talking with the Empress in the Greek language, ancient and modern, both of which she spoke with equal facility.

This might have appeared to be a quaint fancy, but it was explained as soon as the Empress's mental condition was better understood. Haunted by a melancholy past, romantic by temperament and poetic by instinct, she had sought a refuge in literature and the arts. Greece personified in her imagination the land of beauty which her dreams incessantly evoked; she had a passionate love for antiquity, loved its artists and its poets; she wanted to be able, everywhere and at all times, when the obsession of her sorrowful memories became too intense, to escape from the pitiless phantoms that pursued her and in some way to isolate her thoughts from the realities of life. The scholarly conversation of the young Greek *savant* made this effort easier for her; in the varied and picturesque surroundings which her æsthetic tastes demanded, she took Homer and Plato for her companions; and thus to the delight of the eyes was added the most delicate satisfaction of the mind.

The Greek reader, therefore, was the faithful participator in her afternoon walks, which lasted until dusk, and the Empress often covered a distance of fifteen to twenty miles on end. For twenty years, she had obstinately refused to allow herself to be photographed; she dreaded the professional indiscretion of amateur photographers; and no sooner did she perceive a camera aimed in her direction than she quickly unfurled a black feather fan and modestly concealed her face, leaving nothing visible above the feathers but her great, wide, never-to-be-forgotten eyes, which had retained all the splendour and fire of her youth.

The young Greek's duties, however, were not confined to talking to the Empress on her walks. Sometimes the reader would read. Carrying a book which she had selected beforehand, he read a few chapters to her during the rests by the roadside, on the mountain-tops, or at the deserted edge of the sea. Later, he added the daily budget of cuttings from the newspapers and reviews which I prepared for Her Majesty, knowing the interest which she took in the current events of the day.

He also carried on his arm a dark garment—a skirt, in short. The Empress had the habit, in the course of her long walks, of changing the skirt in which she had started for one of a lighter material. It was a question of health and comfort. This little change of attire was effected in the most primitive fashion. The Empress would disappear behind a rock or a tree, while the reader, accustomed to this rapid and discreet proceeding, waited in the road, taking care to look the other way. The Empress handed him the skirt which she had cast off; and the walk was resumed.

On returning to the hotel, she made a frugal dinner, consisting sometimes merely of a bowl of iced milk and some raw eggs washed down with a glass of Tokay, an almost savage dietary to which she had forced herself in order to preserve the slimness of figure which she prized so highly. She took all her meals alone, in a private room, and seldom passed the evening with her suite. Its members hardly ever set eyes on her; sometimes the lady-in-waiting spent day after day without so much as seeing her imperial mistress.

Of the different places in France which Her Majesty visited, the one which she loved above all others was Cap Martin, the promontory which separates the Bay of Monaco from that of Mentone. She came here for three years in succession and returned to it each time with an equal pleasure. The softness of the climate, the wild beauty of the views, the splendour of the luxurious vegetation and the poetic solitude of the pine-forests and orange-groves, reminded her of her property of Achilleon in the island of Corfu and of her palace of Miramar on the shores of the Adriatic. She selected as her residence the enormous hotel that stands at the end of the point, among the tall pines, the fields of rosemary, the clusters of myrtle and arbutus.

The furniture of the imperial apartments was marked by extreme simplicity, combined with perfect taste, most of the pieces being of English workmanship. Her bed-room was just the ordinary hotel bed-room, with a brass bedstead surmounted by a mosquito net, a mahogany dressing-table and a few etchings hanging on the walls. On the other hand, the management had placed beside the bed, at her request, a system of electric bells distinguished by their colours—white, yellow, green and blue, which enabled her to summon that person of her suite whose presence she required, without having to disturb any of the others.

In addition to the ground floor, one other room was reserved for her on every Sunday during her visits. This was the billiard-room, which on that day was transformed into a chapel. When the Empress came to the Cap Martin Hôtel for the first time, she inquired after a church, for she was very religious. There was none in the immediate neighbourhood; to hear mass one had to go to the village of Roquebrune, the parish to which Cap Martin belongs. The Empress then decided to improvise a chapel in the hotel itself and, for this purpose, selected the billiard-room, to which she could repair without attracting attention. But the rites of the Church require that every room in which mass is said should first be consecrated; and none save the bishop of the diocese is qualified to perform the consecration. A ceremony of this kind in an hotel and in a billiard-room would have been rather embarrassing. The difficulty was overcome in a curious and unexpected manner. There is an old rule, by virtue of which the great dignitaries of the religious Order of Malta enjoy the privilege of consecrating any room in which they drop their cloak. It was remembered that General Berzeviczy, the Empress's chamberlain, occupied one of the highest ranks in the knighthood of Malta. He was therefore asked to drop his cloak in the billiard-room. Thenceforward, every Sunday morning, the Empress's footman put up a portable altar in front of the tall oak chimney-piece. He arranged a number of gilt chairs before it; and the old rector of Roquebrune came and said mass, served by a little acolyte to whom the lady-in-waiting handed a gold coin when he went away....

The Empress was extremely generous; and her generosity adopted the most delicate forms. Herself so sad, she wished to see none but happy faces ever about her. And so she always distributed lavish gratuities to all who served her; and she succoured all the poor of the country-side. Whenever, in the course of her walks, she saw some humble cottage hidden in the mountain among the olive-trees, she entered it, talked to the peasants, took the little children on her knees and, as she feared lest the sudden offer of a sum of money might offend those whom she was anxious to assist, she employed the most charming subterfuges. She would ask leave to taste their fruit, paying for it royally ... or else she bought several quarts of milk, or dozens of eggs, which she told them to bring to the hotel next day.

She ended, of course, by knowing all the walks at Cap Martin and the neighbourhood. She set out each morning with her faithful tramping companion, the Greek reader. Sometimes, she would go along the rocks on the shore, sometimes wend her way through the woods; sometimes she would climb the steep hills, scrambling "up to the goats," as the herds say.... She never mentioned the destination or the direction of her excursions, a thing which troubled me greatly, notwithstanding that I had had the whole district searched and explored beforehand. How was I to look after her?

"Set your mind at ease, my dear M. Paoli," she used to say, laughing. "Nothing will happen to me. What would you have them do to a poor woman? Besides, we are no more than the petal of a poppy or a ripple on the water!"

THE EMPRESS OF AUSTRIA

Nevertheless, I was not easy, the more so as she obstinately refused to let one of my men follow her, even at a distance. One evening, however, having heard that some Italian navvies, who were at work on the Mentone road, had spoken in threatening terms of the crowned heads who are in the habit of visiting that part of the country, I begged the Empress to be pleased not to go in that direction and was promptly snubbed for my pains.

"More of your fears," she replied. "I repeat, I am not afraid of them ... and I make no promise."

I was determined. I redoubled my supervision and resolved to send one of my Corsican detectives, fully armed, disguised and got up like a navvy, with instructions to mix with the Italians who were breaking stones on the road. He rigged himself out in a canvas jacket and a pair of corduroy trousers and made up his face to perfection. Speaking Italian fluently, he diverted all suspicion on the part of his mates, who took him for a newly-arrived fellow-countryman of their own.

He was there, lynx-eyed, with ears pricked up, doing his best to break a few stones, when suddenly a figure which he at once recognised appeared at a turn in the road. The night was beginning to fall; the Empress, accompanied by her reader, was on her way back to Cap Martin. Bending over his heap of stones, the sham navvy waited rather anxiously. When the Empress reached the group of road-makers, she stopped, hesitated a moment and then, noticing my man, doubtless because he looked the oldest, went up to him and said, in her kind way:

"Is that hard work you're doing, my good man?"

Not daring to raise his head, he stammered a few words in Italian.

"Don't you speak French?"

"*No, signora.*"

"Have you any children?"

"*Si, signora.*"

"Then take this for them," slipping a louis into his hand. "Tell them that it comes from a lady who is very fond of children." And the Empress walked away.

That same evening, seeing me at the hotel, she came up to me with laughing eyes:

"Well, M. Paoli, you may scold me, if you like. I have been disobedient. I went along the Mentone road to-day and I talked to a navvy."

It was my faithful Corsican.

Sometimes she ventured beyond the radius of her usual walks. For instance, one afternoon she sent for me on returning from a morning excursion:

"M. Paoli, you must be my escort to-day. You shall take me to the Casino at Monte Carlo; I have never been there. I must really, for once in my life, see what a gambling-room is like."

Off we went—the Empress, Countess Sztaray, and myself. It was decided that we should go by train. We climbed into a first-class carriage in which two English ladies were already seated. The Empress, thoroughly enjoying her *incognito*, sat down beside them. At Monte Carlo, we made straight for the Casino and walked into the roulette-room. The august visitor, who had slipped through the crowd of punters leaning over the table, followed each roll of the ball with her eyes, looking as pleased and astonished as a child with a new toy. Suddenly, she took a five-franc piece from her hand-bag:

"Let me see if I have any luck," she said to us. "I believe in number 33."

She put the big coin on number 33 *en plein*. At the first spin of the wheel, it lost. She put on another and lost again. The third time, number 33 turned up. The croupier pushed 175 francs across to her with his rake. She gathered it up, and then, turning gaily to us, said:

"Let us go away quickly. I have never won so much money in my life."

And she dragged us from the Casino.

Whenever she went to Monte Carlo, she never failed to go and have tea at Rumpelmayer, the famous Viennese confectioner's, for, as I have already said, she adored pastry and sweets. The Rumpelmayer establishments at Mentone, Nice and Monte Carlo were well aware of the identity of their regular customer; but she had asked them not to betray her *incognito*. When there were many people in the shop, she would sit down at a little table near the counter; and nobody would have suspected that the simple, comely lady in black, who talked so familiarly with the girls in the pay-box and at the counter, was the Empress of Austria and Queen of Hungary.

3.

The Emperor joined the Empress on three occasions during her visits to Cap Martin. The event naturally created a diversion in the monotony of our sojourn. Though travelling *incognito* as Count Hohenembs, he was accompanied by a fairly numerous suite, whose presence brought a great animation into our little colony. I had, of course, to redouble my measures of protection and to send to Paris for an additional force of detective-inspectors.

Francis Joseph generally spent a fortnight with his consort. I thus had the opportunity of observing the touching affection which they displayed to each other, in spite of the gossip of which certain sections of the press have made themselves the complacent echo. Nothing could be simpler or more charming than their meetings. As soon as the train stopped at Mentone station, where the Empress went to wait its arrival, accompanied by the members of her suite, the Austrian Consul, the Prefect of the Alpes-Maritimes, the Mayor of Mentone and myself, the Emperor sprang lightly to the platform and hastened, bare-headed, to the Empress, whom he kissed on both cheeks. His expressive face, framed in white whiskers, lit up with a kindly smile. He tucked the Empress's arm under his own, and, with an exquisite courtesy, addressed a few gracious words to each of us individually.

During the Emperor's stay, the Empress emerged for a little while from her state of timid isolation. They walked or drove together and received visits from the princes staying on the Côte d'Azur or passing through, notably the Prince of Wales, the Archduke Regnier, the Tsarevitch, the Prince of Monaco, the King and Queen of Saxony and the Grand-duke Michael. Sometimes, they would call on the late Queen of England, at that time installed at Cimiez, or on the Empress Eugénie, their near neighbour. It was like a miniature copy of the Court of Vienna, transferred to Cap Martin.

Francis Joseph, faithful to his habits, rose at five o'clock in the morning and worked with his secretaries. At half-past six, he stopped to take a cup of coffee and then closeted himself once more in his study until ten. The wires were kept working almost incessantly between Cap Martin and Vienna; as many as eighty telegrams have been known to be dispatched and received in the space of a single morning. From ten to twelve, the Emperor strolled in the gardens with the Empress.

Francis Joseph often had General Gebhardt, the Governor of Nice, to dinner and generally took a keen interest in military affairs. When he went to Mentone to return the visit which President Faure had paid him at Cap Martin, the French Government sent a regiment of cuirassiers from Lyons to salute him. The Emperor, struck by the men's fine bearing, reviewed them and watched them march past.

It also occurred to me, during his stay in the south in the spring of 1896, to obtain an opportunity for His Imperial Majesty to witness a sham fight planned by the 87th battalion of Alpine Chasseurs on the height of Roquebrune. The manœuvres opened one morning at dawn in the marvellous circle of hills covered with olive-trees and topped by the snowy summits of the Alps. For two hours, the Emperor followed the incidents of the fight with close attention, not forgetting to congratulate the officers warmly at the finish.

On the next day, he invited the officer in command of the battalion, now General Baugillot, to luncheon. The major was a gallant soldier, who was more accustomed to the language of the camp than to that of courts, and he persisted in addressing the Emperor as "Sire" and "Monsieur" by turns. Francis Joseph smiled, with great amusement. At last, not knowing what to do, the major cried:

"I beg everybody's pardon! I am more used to mess-rooms than drawing-rooms!"

The Emperor at once replied:

"Call me whatever you please. I much prefer a soldier to a courtier."

Cap Martin and Aix were not the only places visited by the Empress of Austria. In the autumn of 1896 she was anxious to see Biarritz; she returned there in the following year and I again had the honour of accompanying her. The inclemency of the weather shortened the stay which she had at first intended to make; and yet the rough and picturesque poetry of the Basque coast had an undoubted attraction for her. She spent her days, sometimes, on the steepest points of the rocks, from which she would watch the tide for hours, often returning soaked through with spray; at other times, she would roam about the wild country that stretches to the foot of the Pyrenees, talking to the Basque peasants and interesting herself in their work.

She had a mania for buying a cow in every district which she visited for the first time. She chose it herself in the course of her walks and had it sent to one of her farms in Hungary. As soon as she saw a cow the colour of whose coat pleased her, she would accost the peasant, ask the animal's price and tell him to take it to her hotel.

One day, near Biarritz, she saw a magnificent black cow, bought it then and there, gave her name of Countess Hohenembs to its owner and sent him to the hotel with her purchase. When he arrived, however, and asked for Countess Hohenembs, the porter, who had not been prepared, took him for a madman and tried to send him away. The peasant insisted, explained what had happened and ended by learning that Countess Hohenembs was no other than the Empress of Austria. An empress? But then he had been cheated! And he began to lament and shout and protest and lose his temper:

"If I had known it was a queen," he yelled, "I'd have asked more money! I must have a bigger price!"

The discussion lasted for two hours and I had to be called to put a stop to it.

This was not the only amusing adventure that occurred during the Empress's stay at Biarritz. One day, returning from an excursion to Fuentarabia, she stood waiting for a train on the platform of the little frontier station at

Hendaye. The reader, who was with her, had gone to ask a question of the station-master. The conversation seemed never-ending and the train arrived. The Empress, losing patience, called a porter:

"You see that gentleman in black?" she said. "Go and tell him to hurry, or the train will leave without us."

The porter ran up to the reader and exclaimed:

"Hurry up, or your wife will go without you!"

The Empress, who rarely laughed, was greatly amused at this incident.

The strange form of neurasthenia from which she suffered, instead of decreasing with time, seemed to become more persistent and more painful as the years went on; and it ended by gradually impairing her health. Not that the Empress had a definite illness—she simply felt an infinite lassitude, a perpetual weariness, against which she tried to struggle, with an uncommon display of energy, by pursuing her active life in spite of it, her wandering life and her long daily walks.

She hated medicine and believed that a sound and simple plan of hygiene was far preferable to any number of doctors' prescriptions. One day, however, seeing her more tired than usual, I begged her permission to present her with a few bottles of Vin Mariani, of the restorative virtues of which I had had personal experience.

"If it gives you any satisfaction," she replied, with a smile, "I accept. But you must let me, in return, send you some of our famous Tokay, which is also a restorative and, moreover, very pleasant to take."

A little while after, Count von Wolkenstein-Trosburg handed me, on behalf of the Empress, a beautiful liqueur-case containing six little bottles of Tokay; and I was talking of drinking it after my meals, like an ordinary dessert-wine, when the count said:

"Do you know that this is a very costly gift? The wine comes direct from the Emperor's estates. To give you an idea of what it is worth, I may tell you that, recently, at a sale in Frankfort, six little bottles fetched eleven thousand francs.... It stands quite alone."

I at once ceased to treat it as a common Madeira. The proprietor of the hotel, hearing of the present which I had received, offered me five thousand francs for the six bottles. I need hardly say that I refused.... I have four bottles left and am keeping them.

Towards the end of the same year, 1897, when she was staying for the second time at Biarritz, the Empress, feeling more restless and melancholy than ever, resolved to make a cruise in the Mediterranean on board her yacht *Miramar*. But she wished first to spend a few days in Paris.

She had engaged a suite of rooms at an hotel in the Rue Castiglione and naturally wanted to preserve the strictest *incognito*. Still, it was known that she was in Paris; and the protection with which I surrounded her was even more rigorous than before. She was out of doors from morning till evening, went through the streets on foot to visit the churches, monuments and museums and at four o'clock called regularly at a dairy in the Rue de Surène, where she was served with a glass of ass's milk, her favourite beverage, after which she returned to the hotel.

One day, however, we had a great alarm; at seven o'clock she was not yet back. I anxiously sent to her sisters, the Queen of Naples and the Countess of Trani, to whom she occasionally paid surprise visits. She was not there. To crown all, she had succeeded in eluding the vigilance of the inspector who was charged to follow her at a certain distance. We had lost the Empress in the midst of Paris! Picture our mortal anxiety!

I was about to set out myself in search of her, when suddenly we saw her very calmly appearing.

"I have been gazing at Notre Dame by moonlight," she said. "It was lovely. And I came back on foot along the quays. I went among the crowd and nobody took the least notice of me."

I remember that her Greek reader, at that time Mr. Barker, and her secretary, Dr. Kromar, expressed a wish to see something of the picturesque and characteristic side of Paris; and I took them one evening to the central markets. When we had finished our visit, I invited them, in accordance with the traditional habit, to come and have a plate of *soupe à l'oignon* in one of the little common eating-houses in the neighbourhood. Delighted with this modest banquet, they described their outing to the Empress next day and sang the praises of our famous national broth, which she had never tasted.

"M. Paoli," she said enthusiastically, "I must know what *soupe à l'oignon* is like. Mr. Barker has given me a most tantalising description."

"Nothing is easier. I will tell the people of the hotel to make you some."

"Never! They will send me up a carefully-prepared soup which won't taste in the least like yours. And I must have it served in the identical crockery. I want all the local colour."

Here I must make a confession: as I had it at heart (it was a question of patriotism, nothing less) that the Empress should not be disappointed, I thought it more prudent to apply to the manager of the hotel, who, kindly lending himself to my innocent fraud, prepared the onion soup and sent to the nearest bazaar for a plate and soup-tureen of the "local colour" in which the imperial traveller took so great an interest. The illusion was perfect. The Empress thought the soup excellent and the crockery delightfully picturesque; true, we had chipped it about a little!

The Empress's only visit to Paris was a short one. As I have said, she had decided that year to air her melancholy on the blue waters of the Mediterranean. The projected cruise embraced a number of calls at different harbours along the Côte d'Azur; and she asked me to accompany her.

We left Paris on the 30th of December for Marseilles, where the imperial yacht lay waiting for us, commanded by a very distinguished officer, Captain Moritz Sacks von Bellenau; and we were at sea, opposite the tragic Château d'If, on the 1st of January of the year 1898, which was to prove so tragic to Elizabeth of Austria. I offered her my wishes for happiness and a long life. The Empress seemed to me sadder and more thoughtful that morning than usual:

"I wish you also," she said, "health and happiness for you and yours." And she added, with an expression of infinite bitterness, "As for myself, I have no confidence left in the future."

Had she already received a presentiment of what the year held in store for her? Who can tell?

She gave us but little of her society during this voyage. She spent her days on deck, and interested herself in the silent activity, in the humble, poetic life of the crew. The sailors entertained a sort of veneration for her. They were constantly feeling the effects of her discreet and delicate kindness. Like ourselves, they respected her melancholy and her love of solitude. And, in the evenings, while the little court collected in the saloon and amused themselves with different games, or else improvised a charming concert; while, at the other end of the ship, the sailors, seated under the poop, sang their Tyrolean or Hungarian songs to an accordion accompaniment, the Empress, all alone on deck, with her eyes staring into the distance, would dream of the stars.

After leaving Marseilles, we went to Villafranca, near Nice, skirting the coast. The Empress also wished to stop at Cannes and to see once more, from the sea, Monaco, Cap Martin and Mentone. She next proposed to revisit Sicily, Greece, and Corfu: it was as though she felt a secret desire to make a sort of pilgrimage to all the ephemeral landmarks which her sad soul had visited in the course of her wandering life.

However enjoyable this cruise might be to me, I had to think of abandoning it. My service with the Empress ended automatically as soon as she had left French waters.

"Stay on, nevertheless," she said kindly. "You shall be my guest; and I will show you my beautiful palace in Corfu."

But my duties, unfortunately, summoned me elsewhere. I had to return to Nice, to receive the King and Queen of Saxony, who were expected there. It was decided, therefore, that I should leave the *Miramar* at San Remo. When the yacht dropped her anchor outside the little Italian town, I said good-bye to the Empress and my charming travelling-companions.

"It will not be for long, for I shall come back to France," said Elizabeth.

She leant over the bulwarks, as the yacht's launch took me on shore, and I watched her delicate and careworn features, first outlined against the disc of the setting sun and then merging, little by little, in the distance and the darkness.

4.

Seven months had elapsed since the day when I left the Empress at San Remo. I was in Paris and read in the papers that she had just arrived at Caux, a picturesque little place situated above Montreux, overlooking the Lake of Geneva. I hastened to write, on chance, to Mr. Barker, her Greek reader, in order to receive news of her. When I came home, on the evening of the 9th of September, I was handed Mr. Barker's reply, in which was conveyed news of the Empress's plans, and a gracious invitation from her to visit her, should I happen to be in the neighbourhood of Geneva.

As I was on leave and had nothing to keep me in Paris, I at once made up my mind and, the next morning, took the train for Geneva. I calculated that, arriving in the evening, I had a chance of still finding the Empress at the Hôtel Beau Rivage; besides, nothing need prevent me from going the next morning to Caux, where I was sure to see her, and, at the same time, to be able to shake hands with General Berzeviczy and Mr. Barker. Who would have thought that the train which carried me through the green fields of Burgundy and Franche-Comté was taking me straight to the scene of a sad and blood-stained tragedy?

When we drew into the station at Geneva, I noticed an unwonted animation on the platforms; groups of people stood about in excited discussion, with a look of consternation on their faces. I paid no particular attention, however, for I was in a hurry. I hailed a fly and told the man to drive to the Hôtel Beau Rivage. We had not gone twenty yards when he turned round on his box:

THE EMPEROR AND EMPRESS OF AUSTRIA

"What an awful crime!" he said.

"What crime?"

"Haven't you heard? The Empress was murdered this afternoon."

"Murdered!"

Livid and scared, I could hardly listen to the pitiful story of the tragedy. The Empress, it seemed, had been stabbed to the heart by an Italian anarchist when about to embark on the 1:40 steamer for Territet; she sank down on the Quai du Mont Blanc. The people around her thought that she had fainted, and carried her on board the boat; when they bent over her, she was dead.

I sprang quickly from the carriage, when it pulled up at the hotel, rushed into the hall, which was full of people, flew up the crowded staircase and along a corridor in which English, German and Russian travellers were hustling one another, with scared faces, all anxious to see. At last, catching sight of a servant:

"Countess Sztaray?" I asked.

"In there," he replied, pointing to a door standing ajar.

I knocked, the door was opened and Countess Sztaray, red-eyed, her features distorted with grief, gave me a heart-broken look and, with a sob, said:

"Our poor Empress!"

"Where is she?"

"Come with me."

Taking me by the hand, she led me and General Berzeviczy, who had also just arrived, to the next room. There lay the Empress, stiff and already cold, stretched on a little brass bed under a thin, white gauze veil. Her face, lit up by the flickering flame of two tall candles, showed no trace of suffering. A sad smile still seemed to hover over her pale and lightly-parted lips; two long tresses fell upon her slim shoulders; the delicate features of her face had shrunk; two purple shadows under her eyelids threw into relief the sharp outline of her nose and the pallor of her cheeks.

She appeared as though sleeping peacefully and happily. Her tiny hands were crossed over an ivory crucifix; some roses, already almost withered—roses which she had gathered that morning and which she was carrying in her arms when she received her death-blow—lay scattered at her feet.

I stood long contemplating the corpse. My self-possession deserted me. In spite of myself, the tears came to my eyes, and I cried like a child.

.   .   .   .

Why had fate decreed that the Empress should go to Geneva? Curiously enough, the idea came to her suddenly, it appeared, on Thursday, the 8th of September. She had arranged to pay a visit to her friend, Baronne Adolphe de Rothschild, who was staying at her country house, the Château de Pregny, at the western end of the lake. But it was a long excursion to make in a single day; and the Empress, contrary to the advice of Countess Sztaray, decided to sleep at Geneva, after leaving Pregny, and not to return to Caux until the following afternoon. She arrived at the Hôtel Beau Rivage in the evening and went out after dinner. She was up the next day at five o'clock. After filling a portion of her morning with the complicated cares of her toilet and her correspondence, she went for a walk along the shady quays of the Rhone. Returning to the hotel at one o'clock, she hurriedly drank a glass of milk. Then, accompanied by her lady-in-waiting, Countess Sztaray, she hastened down to the steamboat pier, intending to take the Territet boat that started at 1:40. She had come to within two hundred yards of the footplank connecting the steamer with the Quai du Mont Blanc, when Lucchini flung himself upon her and struck her a blow under the left breast with a three-cornered file clumsily fitted to a wooden handle. The violence of the blow broke her fourth rib.

Death was not instantaneous. She had the strength to walk as far as the boat and for this reason: the instrument, in its course, had pierced the left ventricle of the heart from top to bottom. But, the blade being very sharp and very thin, the hemorrhage at first was almost insignificant. The drops of blood escaped very slowly from the heart; and its action was not impaired so long as the pericardium, in which the drops were collecting, was not full. This was how she was able to go a fairly long distance on foot with a stab in her heart. When the bleeding increased, the Empress sank to the deck.

The poor Empress, therefore, had the energy to drag herself to the boat, where a band of gipsies was playing Hungarian dances (a cruel irony of chance), while the steamer began to move away from the landing-stage. At that moment, she fainted. Countess Sztaray, who believed her to be stunned by a blow of the fist—for no one had seen the weapon in the assassin's hand—tried to bring her to with smelling-salts. The Empress, in fact, recovered consciousness, spoke a few words, cast a long look of bewildered astonishment around her and then, suddenly, fell back dead. The dismay and excitement were intense. The boat at once put back to the pier; and, as there was no litter at hand, the body was carried to the hotel, shrouded in sails, on an improvised bier of crossed oars.

Had the Empress received a presentiment of her tragic end, which a gipsy at Wiesbaden, and a fortune-teller at Corfu had foretold her in the past? Two strange incidents incline one to think so. On the eve of her departure for Geneva, she asked Mr. Barker to read her a few chapters of a book by Marion Crawford, entitled "Corleone," in which the author describes the abominable customs of the Sicilian Mafia. While the Empress was listening to this harrowing story, a raven, attracted by the scent of some fruit which she was eating, came and circled round her. Greatly impressed, she tried to drive it off, but in vain, for it constantly returned, filling the echoes with its mournful croaking. Then she swiftly walked away, for she knew that ravens are harbingers of death when their ill-omened wings persist in flapping around a living person.

Again, Countess Sztaray told me that, on the morning of that day, she went into the Empress's room, as usual, to ask how she had slept, and found her imperial mistress looking pale and sad.

"I have had a strange experience," said Elizabeth. "I was awakened in the middle of the night by the bright moonbeams which filled my room, for the servants had forgotten to draw the blinds. I could see the moon from my bed; and it seemed to have the face of a woman weeping. I don't know if it is a presentiment, but I have an idea that I shall meet with misfortune."

During the three days that preceded the departure of the remains for Vienna,

I stayed at Geneva and shared the funeral watches with the little court, once so happy and now so pitifully robbed of its mistress. General Berzeviczy, Countess Sztaray and I sat for long hours conjuring up the memory of her who was now sleeping her last sleep beside us. Countless anecdotes were told, countless tiny and charming details. It already seemed almost a distant past which we were recalling for the last time, a bright and exquisite past which the gracious Empress was taking away with her.

I went to see the murderer in his cell. I found a perfectly lucid being, boasting of his crime as of an act of heroism. When I asked him what motive had driven him to choose for his victim a woman, a sovereign living as far removed as possible from politics and the throne, one who had always shown so much compassion for the humble and the destitute:

"I struck at the first crowned head," he said, "that came along. I don't care. I wanted to make a manifestation and I have succeeded."

The unhappy Empress's destiny was to be strange and romantic until the end, until after her death. Her body, carried to an hotel bed-room, departed for Austria without pomp or display, amid an immense and silent crowd. The Swiss Government had not the necessary time to levy a regiment to show her the last honours.

But it was better so, for she had, as her escort, a respectfully contemplative nation and, as her salute, the bells of all the towns and all the villages through which the funeral train passed. And this, I am certain, was just the simple and poetic homage which her heart would have desired.

. . . .

A few days after the tragedy, the Emperor Francis Joseph deigned to remember my respectful attachment to the consort whom he had loved so well; and I received the following telegram:

WIENBURG, September 15th, 1898.

To Monsieur Paoli, Ministry of the Interior, Paris,—

His Majesty the Emperor, greatly touched by your sincere sympathy, remembers gratefully the devoted care which you showed the late Empress and thanks you again with all his heart.

PAAR.

Principal Aide-de-camp to H. M. the Emperor of Austria.

I also received from the archduchesses, the daughters, a hunting-knife which their mother, the poor Empress, valued most particularly. I keep it religiously in my little museum. Sometimes I take it out and look at it; and it invariably summons up one of the most touching memories of my life.

II

KING ALFONSO XIII

1.

"You wanted me to complete your collection, didn't you, M. Paoli?"

The presidential train had left Hendaye; the distant echoes of the Spanish national anthem still reached our ears through the silence and the darkness. Leaning from the window of the sleeping-car, I was watching the last lights of the little frontier-town disappear one by one.

I turned round briskly at the sound of that gay and bright voice. A tall, slim young man stood at the door of the compartment, with a cigarette between his lips and a soft felt hat on his head, and gave me a friendly little wave of the hand. His long, slender figure looked very smart and supple in a pale-grey travelling-suit; and a broad smile lit up his bronzed face, his smooth, boyish face, adorned with a large Bourbon hooked nose, planted like an eagle's beak between two very black eyes, full of fire and humour.

"Yes, yes, M. Paoli, I know you, though perhaps you don't yet know me. My mother has often spoken to me of you and, when she heard that you had been appointed to watch over my safety, she said, 'With Paoli, I feel quite at ease.'"

"I am infinitely touched and flattered, Sir," I replied, "by that gracious mark of confidence. It is true that my collection was incomplete without your Majesty."

That is how I became acquainted with H. M. Alfonso XIII, in the spring of 1905, at the time of his first official visit to France. "The little king", as he was still called, had lately completed his nineteenth year. He had attained his majority a bare twelve-month before and was just entering upon his career as a monarch, if I may so express myself. The watchful eyes of Europe were beginning to observe with sympathetic interest the first actions of this young ruler who, with the exuberant grace of his fine and trusting youth, brought an unexpected and amusing contrast into the somewhat constrained formality of the gallery of sovereigns. Though he had no history as yet, plenty of anecdotes were already current about him and a plenty of morals were drawn in consequence:

"He has a nature all impulse," said one.

"He is full of character," said people who had met him.

"He is like his father: he would charm the bird from the tree," an old Spanish diplomatist remarked to me.

"At any rate, there is nothing commonplace about him," thought I, still perplexed by the unconventional, amusing, jocular way in which he had interrupted my nocturnal contemplations.

No, he was certainly not commonplace! The next morning, I saw him at early dawn at the windows of the saloon-carriage, devouring with a delighted curiosity the sights that met his eyes as the train rushed at full speed through the verdant plains of the Charente. Nothing escaped his youthful enthusiasm: fields, forests, rivers, things, people. Everything gave rise to sparkling exclamations:

"What a lovely country yours is, M. Paoli!" he cried, when he saw me standing near him. "I feel as if I were still at home, as if I knew everybody: the faces all seem familiar. It's 'stunning'!"

At the sound of this typically Parisian expression (the French word which he employed was *épatant*) proceeding from the royal lips, it was my turn to be "stunned." In my innocence, I was not yet aware that he knew all our smart slang phrases and used them freely.

His spirits were as inexhaustible as his bodily activity; and, upon my word, we were hard put to it to keep up with him. Now running from one window to another, so as to "miss nothing," as he said, with a laugh; now leaning over the back of a chair or swinging his legs from a table; now striding up and down the carriage, with his hands in his pockets and the everlasting cigarette between his lips, he questioned us without ceasing. He wanted to know everything, though he knew a great deal as it was. The army and navy excited his interest in the highest degree; the provinces through which we were passing, their customs, their past, their administrative organisation, their industries supplied him with the subjects of an exhaustive interrogatory, to which we did our best to reply. Our social laws, our parliament, our politicians as eagerly aroused his lively curiosity, and then came the turn of Paris which he was at last about to see, whose splendours and peculiarities he already knew from reading and hearsay, that Paris which he looked upon as a fairyland, a promised land; and the thought that he was to be solemnly welcomed there sent a slight flush of excitement to his cheeks.

"It must be wonderful!" he said, his eyes ablaze with pleasurable impatience.

He also insisted upon our giving him full details about the persons who were to receive him:

"What is M. Loubet like? And the prime minister? And the governor of Paris?"

When he was not putting questions, he was telling stories, recalling his impressions of his recent journeys in Spain.

"Confess, M. Paoli," he said, "that you have never had to look after a king as young as I."

His conversation, jesting and serious by turns, studded with judicious reflexions, with smart sallies, with freakish outbursts and unexpected digressions, revealed a young and keen intelligence, eager after knowledge, a fresh mind open to effusive ideas, a quivering imagination, counterbalanced, however, by a reflective brain. I remember the astonishment of the French officers who had come to meet him at the frontier, on hearing him discuss matters of military strategy with the authority and the expert wisdom of an old tactician; I remember also the surprise of a high official who had joined the train midway and to whose explanations the King was lending an attentive ear when we crossed a bridge over the Loire, in which some waterfowl happened to be disporting themselves.

"Oh, what a pity!" the King broke in. "Why haven't I a gun?" And, taking aim with an imaginary fowling-piece, "What a fine shot!"

Again, I remember the spontaneous and charming way in which, full of admiration for the beauties of our Touraine, he tapped me on the shoulder and cried:

"There's no doubt about it, I love France! France forever!"

What was not my surprise, afterwards, at Orleans, where the first official stop was made, to see him appear in his full uniform as captain-general, his features wearing an air of singular dignity, his gait proud and lofty, compelling in all of us a respect for the impressive authority that emanated from his whole person! He found the right word for everybody, was careful of the least shades of etiquette, moved, talked and smiled amid the gold-laced uniforms with a sovereign ease, showing from the first that he knew better than anybody how to play his part as a king.

THE KING OF SPAIN, PRINCESS HENRY OF BATTENBERG, PRINCESS VICTORIA EUGENIA AND M. PAOLI

There is one action, very simple in appearance, but in reality more difficult than one would think, by which we can judge a sovereign's bearing in a foreign country. This is his manner of saluting the colours. Some, as they pass before the standard surrounded by its guard of honour, content themselves with raising their hand to their cap or helmet; others stop and bow; others, lastly, make a wide and studied gesture which betrays a certain, almost theatrical affectation. Alfonso XIII's salute is like none of these: in its military stiffness, it is at once simple and grave, marked by supreme elegance and profound deference. On the platform of the Orleans railway-station, opposite the motionless battalion, in the presence of a number of officers and civil functionaries, this salute which so visibly paid a delicate homage to the army and the country, the graceful and respectful salute moved and flattered us more than any number of boasts and speeches. And, when, at last, I went home, after witnessing the young King's arrival in the capital and noticing the impression which he had made on the government and the people, I recalled the old Spanish diplomatist's remark:

"The King would charm the bird from the tree!"

2.

I saw little of King Alfonso during his first stay in Paris. The protection of sovereigns who are the official guests of the government did not come within the scope of my duties. I therefore left him at the station and was not to resume my place in his suite until the moment of his departure. The anarchist revolutionary gentry appeared to be unaware of this detail, for I daily received a fair number of anonymous letters, most of which contained more or less vague threats against the person of our royal visitor. One of them, which the post brought me as I was on the point of proceeding to the gala performance given at the Opera in his honour, struck me more particularly because of the plainness of the warning which it conveyed, a warning devoid of any of the insults that usually accompany this sort of communication:

"In spite of all the precautions that have been taken," it read, "the King had better be careful when he leaves the Opera to-night."

This note, written in a rough, disguised hand, was, of course, unsigned. I at once passed it on to the right quarter. The very strict supervision that was being exercised no doubt excluded the possibility of a successful plot. But there remained the danger of an individual attempt, the murderous act of a single person: and I knew by experience that, to protect one's self against that, one must rely exclusively upon "the police of Heaven," to use the picturesque expression of Señor Maura, the Spanish premier.

Haunted by a baneful presentiment, I nevertheless decided on leaving the Opera, to remain near the King's carriage (as a mere passer-by, of course) until he had stepped into it with M. Loubet and driven off, surrounded by his squadron of cavalry. The attempt on his life took place at the corner of the Rue de Rohan and the Rue de Rivoli; and both the King and M. Loubet enjoyed a miraculous escape from death. My presentiment, therefore, had not been at fault.

I need not here recall the coolness which the young monarch displayed in these circumstances, for it is still present in every memory, nor the magnificent indifference with which he looked upon the tragic incident:

"I have received my baptism of fire," he said to me, a couple of days later, "and, upon my word, it was much less exciting than I expected!"

Alfonso XIII, in fact, has a fine contempt for danger. Like the late King Humbert, he considers that assassination is one of the little drawbacks attendant on the trade of king. He gave a splendid proof of this courage at the time of the Madrid bomb, of which I shall speak later; and I was able to see it for myself two days after the attempted assassination in the Rue de Rohan.

On leaving Paris, our royal visitor went to Cherbourg, where I accompanied him, to embark on board the British royal yacht, which was to take him to England. As we approached the town in the early morning, the presidential train was shunted on to the special line that leads direct to the dockyard. Suddenly, while we were running pretty fast, a short stop took place, producing a violent shock in all the carriages. The reader can imagine the excitement. The railway-officials, officers and chamberlains of the court sprang out on the permanent way and rushed to the royal saloon.

"Another attempt?" asked the King, calmly smiling, as he put his head out of the window.

We all thought so at the first moment. Fortunately, it was only a slight accident: the rear luggage-van had left the rails through a mistake in the shunting. I hastened to explain the matter to the King.

"You'll see," he at once replied, "they will say, all the same, that it was an attempt on my life: I must let my mother know quickly, or she will be frightened."

The King was right. Someone, we never discovered who, had already found means to telegraph to Queen Maria Christina that a fresh attack had been made on her son. There are always plenty of bearers of ill-news, even where sovereigns are concerned and especially when the news is false!

I took leave of the King at Cherbourg and joined him, the week after, at Calais, whence I was to accompany him to the Spanish frontier, for he was returning direct to his own country. This time, the official journey was over; and I once more found the pleasant, simple young man, in the pale-grey suit and the soft hat. The warm welcome which he had received in England had not wiped out his enthusiastic recollection of France.

"By George," he declared, "how glad I am to see this beautiful country again, even through the windows of the railway-carriage!"

A violent shower set in as we left Calais. The train went along a line in process of repair and had to travel very slowly. At that moment, seeing some gangs of navvies working under the diluvial downpour and soaked to the skin, the King leant out of the window and, addressing them:

"Wait a bit!" he said. "I'm going to give you something to smoke. This will warm you."

And the King, after emptying the contents of his cigarette-case into their horny hands, took the boxes of cigars and cigarettes that lay on the tables, one after the other and passed them through the window, first to the delighted labourers and then to the soldiers drawn up on either side of the line. They had never known such a windfall: it rained Upmanns, Henry Clays and Turkish cigarettes. When none were left, the King appealed to the members of his suite, whom he laughingly plundered for the benefit of these decent fellows. They, not knowing his quality, shouted gaily:

"Thank you, sir, thank you! Come back soon!"

We had but one regret, that of remaining without anything to smoke until we were able, at the next stop, to replenish our provisions of tobacco which had been exhausted in so diverting a fashion.

When, on the following morning, we reached Hendaye, which is the frontier station between France and Spain, a very comical incident occurred that amused the young traveller greatly. By a purely fortuitous coincidence, they were waiting, as we pulled up, for the train of King Carlos of Portugal, who was also about to pay an official visit to France; and the authorities and troops had collected on the platform in order to show the usual honours to their new guest. Our sudden arrival, for which nobody was prepared, as Alfonso XIII was not now travelling officially, utterly disconcerted the resplendent crowd. Would the King of Spain think that they were there on his account and would he not be offended when he discovered his mistake? It was a difficult position, but the prefect rose to the occasion. As the King of Portugal's train was not yet signalled, he gave orders to pay the honours to King Alfonso XIII.

The moment, therefore, that our train stopped, the authorities and general officers hurried in our direction and the band of the regiment, which had been practising the Portuguese royal anthem, briskly struck up the Spanish anthem instead. But the King, who knew what he was about, leant from the window and chaffingly cried:

"Please, gentlemen, please! I know that you are not here for me, but for my next-door neighbour!"

At Irun, the first Spanish station, where I was to take leave of our guest, a fresh surprise awaited us. There was not a trace of police-protection, not a soldier, not a gendarme. An immense crowd had freely invaded both platforms. And what a crowd! Thousands of men, women and children shouted, sang, waved their hands, hustled one another and fired guns into the air for joy, while the King, calm and smiling elbowed his way from the presidential to the royal train, patting the children's heads as he passed, paying a compliment to their mothers, distributing friendly nods to the men who were noisily cheering him. And I thought of our democratic country, in which we imprison the rulers of States in an impenetrable circle of police-supervision, whereas here, in a monarchical country, labouring under a so-called reign of terror, the sovereign walks about in the midst of strangers, unprotected by any precautionary measures. It was a striking contrast.

But my mission was at an end. Still laughing, the King, as he gave me his hand, said:

"Well, M. Paoli, you can no longer say that you haven't got me in your collection!"

"I beg your pardon, Sir," I replied. "It's not complete yet."

"How do you mean?"

"Why, Sir, I haven't your portrait."

"Oh, that will be all right!" And, turning to the grand master of his court, "Santo Mauro, make a note: photo for M. Paoli."

A few days after, I received a photograph, signed and dated by the royal hand.

Five months later, Alfonso XIII, returning from Germany, where he had been to pay his accession-visit to the Berlin Court, stopped to spend a day incognito in Paris. I found him as I had left him; gay, enthusiastic, full of good-nature, glad to be alive.

"Here I am again, my dear M. Paoli," he said, when he perceived me at the frontier, where, according to custom, I had gone to meet him. "But this time

I shall not cause you any great worry. I must go home and I sha'n't stop for more than twenty-four hours—worse luck!—in Paris."

On the other hand, he wasted none of his time while there. Jumping into a motor-car the moment he was out of the train, he first drove to the Hôtel Bristol, where he remained just long enough to change his clothes, after which he managed, during his brief stay, to hear mass in the church of St. Roch, for it was Sunday, to pay a visit to M. Loubet, to make some purchases in the principal shops, to lunch with his aunt, the Infanta Eulalie, to take a motor-drive, in the pouring rain, as far as Saint-Germain and back, to dine at the Spanish Embassy and to wind up the evening at the Théâtre des Variétés.

"And it's like that every day, when he's travelling," said one of his suite to me.

The King, I may say, makes up for this daily expenditure of activity with a tremendous appetite. I have observed, for that matter, that the majority of sovereigns are valiant trenchermen. Every morning of his life, Alfonso XIII has a good rumpsteak and potatoes for his first breakfast, often preceded by eggs and sometimes followed by salad and fruit. The King, on the other hand, never drinks wine and generally confines himself to a tumbler of water and *zucharillos*, the national beverage, composed of white of egg beaten up with sugar.

In spite of his continual need of movement, his passionate love of sport in all its forms and especially of motoring, his expansive, rather mad, but very attractive youthfulness, Alfonso XIII, even in his flying trips, never, as we have seen, loses the occasion of improving his mind. He is very quick at seizing a point, possesses a remarkable power of assimilation and, although he does not read much, for he has no patience, he is remarkably well-informed as regards the smallest details that interest him. One day, for instance, he asked me, point-blank:

"Do you know how many gendarmes there are in France?"

I confess that I was greatly puzzled what to reply, for I have never cared much about statistics. I, therefore, ventured, on the off-chance, to say:

"Ten thousand."

"Ten thousand! Come, M. Paoli, what are you thinking of? That's the number we have in Spain. It's more like twenty thousand."

This figure, as I afterwards learnt, was strictly accurate.

As for business of State, I also noticed that the King devoted more time to it than his restless life would lead one to believe. Rising winter and summer at six o'clock, he stays indoors and works regularly during the early portion of the morning and often again at night. In this connexion, one of his ministers said to me:

"He never shows a sign of either weariness or boredom. The King's 'frivolity' is a popular fallacy. On the contrary, he is terribly painstaking. Just like the Queen Mother, he insists upon clear and detailed explanations, before signing the least document; and he knows quite well how to make his will felt. Besides, he is fond of work and he can work no matter where: in a motor-car, in a boat, in the train, as well as in his study."

But it was especially on the occasion of the event which was to mark an indelible date in his life, a fair and happy date, that I had time to observe him and to come to know him better. The reader will have guessed that I am referring to his engagement. The duties which I fulfilled during a quarter of a century have sometimes involved difficult moments, delicate responsibilities, thankless tasks, but they have also procured me many charming compensations; and I have no more delightful recollection than that of witnessing, at first hand, the fresh and touching royal idyll, the simple, cloudless romance, which began one fine evening in London, was subsequently continued under the sunny sky of the Basque coast and ended by leading to one of those rare unions which satisfy the exigencies both of public policy and of the heart.

Like his father before him, Alfonso XIII, when his ministers began to hint discreetly about possible "alliances," contented himself with replying:

"I shall marry a princess who takes my fancy and nobody else. I want to love my wife."

Nevertheless, diplomatic intrigues fashioned themselves around the young sovereign. The Emperor William would have liked to see a German princess sharing the throne of Spain; a marriage with an Austrian archduchess would have continued a time-honoured tradition; the question of a French princess was also mooted, I believe. But the political *rapprochement* between Spain and England had just been accomplished under French auspices; an Anglo-Spanish marriage seemed to correspond with the interests of Spain; and it so happened that the Princess Patricia of Connaught had lately been seen in Andalusia. Her name was on all men's lips; already, in the silence of the palace, official circles were preparing for this union. Only one detail had been omitted, but it was a detail of the first importance: that of consulting the two persons directly interested, who did not even know each other.

When the King went to England, no one thought for a moment but that he would return engaged—and engaged to Patricia of Connaught. The diplomatists, however, had reckoned without a factor, which, doubtless, was foreign to them, but which was all-powerful in the eyes of Alfonso XIII: the little factor known as love.

As a matter of fact, when the two young people met, they did not attract each other. On the other hand, at the ball given in the King's honour at Buckingham Palace, Alfonso never took his eyes off a young, fair-haired princess, whose radiant beauty shed all the glory of spring around her.

"Who is that?" asked the King.

"Princess Ena of Battenberg," was the reply.

The two were presented, danced and talked together, met again on the next day and on the following days.

And, when the King returned to Spain, he left his heart in England.

But he did not breathe a word about it. His little idyll, which took the form of an interchange of letters and postcards as well as of secret negotiations with a view to marriage—negotiations conducted with the English royal family by the King in person—was pursued in the greatest mystery. People knew, of course, that the princess and the King liked and admired each other; but they knew nothing of the young monarch's private plans. Moreover, he took a pleasure in mystifying his entourage. He who had once been so expansive now became suddenly contemplative and reserved.

Soon after his return, he ordered a yacht; and, when the time came to christen her, he made the builders paint on the prow in gold letters:

PRINCESS ...

The comment aroused by these three little dots may be easily imagined.

The moment, however, was at hand when the name of the royal yacht's godmother and, therefore, of the future Queen of Spain was to be revealed. One morning in January, 1906, I received a letter from Miss Minnie Cochrane, Princess Henry of Battenberg's faithful lady-in-waiting, telling me that the princess and her daughter, Princess Ena, were leaving shortly for Biarritz, to stay with their cousin, the Princess Frederica of Hanover, and inviting me to accompany them. This kind thought is explained by the fact that I had known the princess and her daughter for many years: I had often had occasions to see Princess Beatrice with the late Queen Victoria, to whom she showed the most tender filial affection; I had also known Princess Ena as a little girl, when she still wore short frocks and long fair curls and used to play with her doll under the fond, smiling gaze of her august grandmother. She was then a grave and reflective child; she had great, deep, expressive blue eyes; and she was a little shy, like her mother.

When at Calais, I beheld a fresh and beautiful young girl, unreserved and gay, a real fairy princess, whose face, radiant with gladness, so evidently reflected a very sweet, secret happiness; when, on the day after her arrival at Biarritz, I unexpectedly saw King Alfonso arrive in a great state of excitement and surprised the first glance which they exchanged at the door of the villa, then I understood. I was, therefore, not in the least astonished when Miss Cochrane, whom I had ventured to ask if it was true that there was a matrimonial project on foot between the King and the princess, answered, with a significant smile:

"I think so; it is not officially settled yet; it will be decided here."

3.

The Villa Mouriscot, where the princesses were staying, was a picturesque Basque chalet, elegantly and comfortably furnished. Standing on a height, at two miles from Biarritz, whence the eye commanded the magnificent circle of hills, and buried in the midst of luxuriant and fragrant gardens, intersected by shady and silent walks, it formed an appropriately poetic setting for the romance of the royal betrothal.

The King came every day. Wrapped in a huge cloak, with a motoring-cap and goggles, he would arrive at ten o'clock in the morning from San Sebastian in his double Panhard, which he drove himself, except on the rare occasions when he entrusted the steering-wheel to his excellent French chauffeur, Antonin, who accompanied him on all his excursions. His friends, the Marquis de Viana, the young Conde de Villalobar, counsellor to the Spanish Embassy in London, Señor Quiñones de Leon, the charming attaché to the Paris Embassy, the Conde del Grove, his faithful aide-de-camp, or the Marquis de Pacheco, commanding the palace halberdiers, formed his usual suite. As soon as the motor had passed through the gates and stopped before the door, where Baron von Pawel-Rammingen, the Princess Frederica's husband, and Colonel Lord William Cecil, Princess Henry of Battenberg's comptroller, awaited him, the King hurried to the drawing-room, where the pretty princess sat looking out for his arrival, as impatient for the meeting as the King himself.

After the King had greeted his hosts at the villa, he and the princess walked into the gardens and exchanged much lively talk as they strolled about the paths in which, as Gounod's song says, "lovers lose their way." They returned in time for the family lunch, a very simple repast to which the King's tremendous appetite did full honour. He used often to send for Fraülein Zinska, the Princess Frederica's old Hanoverian cook, and congratulate her on her culinary capacities, a proceeding which threw the good woman into an ecstasy of delight. After lunch, the young people, accompanied by Miss Cochrane as chaperone, went out in the motor, not returning until nearly dark. On rainy days, of course, there was no drive; but in the drawing-room of the villa the Princess Frederica had thoughtfully contrived a sort of recess, furnished with a sofa, in which the engaged couple could pursue their discreet flirtation at their ease. When they took refuge there, the young Prince Alexander of Battenberg, who had joined his family at Biarritz, used to tease them:

THE KING AND QUEEN OF SPAIN AND BABY

"Look out!" he would cry to anyone entering the room. "Be careful! Don't disturb the lovers!"

In the evening, at dinner, the suite were present. The King changed into evening-clothes, with the collar of the Golden Fleece. At half-past ten, he left for the station and returned to San Sebastian by the Sud-Express.

After a few days, although they were not officially engaged, no one doubted that the event was near at hand.

"She's nice, isn't she?" the King asked me, point-blank.

A significant detail served to show me how far things had gone. One day, the two young people, accompanied by the Princesses Frederica and Beatrice and the whole little court, walked to the end of the grounds, to a spot near the lake, where two holes had been newly dug. A gardener stood waiting for them, carrying two miniature fir-plants in his arms.

"This is mine," said the King.

"And this is mine," said the princess, in French, for they constantly spoke French together.

"We must plant the trees side by side," declared the King, "so that they may always remind us of these never-to-be-forgotten days."

No sooner said than done. In accordance with the old English tradition, the two of them, each laying hold of a spade, dug up the earth and heaped it around the shrubs with shouts of laughter that rang clear through the silent wood. Then, when the King, who, in spite of his strength of arm, is a poor gardener, perceived that the princess had finished her task first:

"There is no doubt about it," he said, "I am very awkward! I must put in a month or two with the Engineers!"

On returning to the villa, he gave the princess her first present: a heart set in brilliants. It was certainly a day of symbols.

On the following day, things took a more definite turn. The King came to fetch the princesses in the morning to take them to San Sebastian, where they met Queen Maria Christina. Nobody knew what happened in the course of the interview and the subsequent private luncheon at the Miramar Palace. But it was, beyond a doubt, a decisive day. At Fuentarabia, the first Spanish town through which they passed on their way to San Sebastian in the morning, the King said to the princess:

"You are now on Spanish soil."

"Oh," she said, "I am so glad!"

"It will soon be for good."

And they smiled to each other.

The frantic cheering that greeted her entry at San Sebastian, the hail of flowers that fell at her feet when she passed through the streets, the motherly kiss with which she was received at the door of Queen Maria Christina's drawing-room must have given Princess Ena to understand that all Spain had confirmed its sovereign's choice and applauded his good taste.

Twenty-four hours after this visit, the Queen Mother, in her turn, went to Biarritz and took tea at the Villa Mouriscot. The King had gone on before her. Intense happiness was reflected on every face. When the Queen, who had very graciously sent for me to thank me for the care which I was taking of her son, stepped into her carriage, she said to the princess, with a smile:

"We shall soon see you in Madrid."

Then, taking a white rose from the bouquet with which the Mayor of Biarritz had presented her, she gave it to the princess, who pressed it to her lips before pinning it to her bodice.

That same evening, the King, beaming all over his face, cried to me from a distance, the moment he saw me:

"It's all right, Paoli; the official demand has been granted. You see before you the happiest of men!"

He was indeed happy, so much so that his gaiety infected everybody around him. Each of us felt that he had some small part in this frank happiness, in this touching romance; and we felt all its charm as though our hearts were but twenty years old again. The English themselves, forgetting that their princess was about to marry a Catholic sovereign and that she would have to forswear the Protestant faith—an essential condition of the marriage—the English, usually so strict in these matters, greeted this love-match with enthusiasm. One of the British ministers gave vent to a very pretty phrase. Someone expressing surprise, in his presence, at the acquiescence shown in this connexion by King Edward's government:

"Mankind loves a lover," he replied. "Especially in England."

The days that followed upon the betrothal were days of enchantment for the young couple, now freed from all preoccupation and constraint. One met them daily, motoring along the picturesque roads of the Basque country or walking through the streets of Biarritz, stopping before the shopwindows, at the photographer's or at the pastrycook's.

"Do you know, Paoli," said the King to me, one day, "I've changed the princess's name. Instead of calling her Ena, which I don't like, I call her Nini. That's very Parisian, isn't it?"

The royal lover, as I have already said, prided himself with justice on his Parisianism, as witness the following scrap of dialogue, which took place one morning in the street at Biarritz:

"M. Paoli."

"Sir?"

"Do you know the tune of the *Maschich*?"

"Upon my word, I can't say I do, Sir!"

"Or of *Viens, Poupoule*?"

"No, Sir."

"Why, then you know nothing. Paoli ... you're a disgrace!"

Thereupon, half-opening the door of the confectioner's shop where Princess Ena was making a leisurely selection of cakes, he began to hum the famous air of *Viens, Poupoule*!

It will readily be imagined that the protection of the King was not always an easy matter. True, it was understood that I should invariably be told beforehand of the programme of the day; but the plans would be changed an hour later; and, when the young couple had once set out at random, nothing was more difficult than to catch them up.

I remember one morning when the King informed me that he did not intend to go out that day. I thereupon determined to give myself a few hours' rest. I had returned to my hotel and was beginning to enjoy the unaccustomed sense of repose when the telephone bell rang:

"The King and the Princess have gone out," said the voice of one of my detectives. "It's impossible to find them."

Greatly alarmed, I was hurrying to the Villa Mouriscot, when, at a bend in the road, I saw the fugitives themselves before me, accompanied by the Princess Beatrice.

"I say!" cried the King, in great glee. "We gave your inspector the slip!"

And, as I was venturing to utter a discreet reproach:

"Don't be angry with us, M. Paoli," the princess broke in, very prettily. "The King isn't frightened; no more am I. Who would think of hurting us?"

The great delight of Alfonso, who is very playfully inclined, was to hoax people that did not know who he was. One day, motoring into Cambo, the delicious village near which M. Edmond Rostand's property lies, he entered the post-office to send off some postcards. Seeing the woman in charge of the office taking the air outside the door:

"I beg your pardon, madame," he said, very politely. "Could you tell me if the King of Spain is expected here to-day?"

"I don't know anything about it," said the little post-mistress in an off-hand way.

"Don't you know him by sight?"

"No."

"Oh, really! They say he's very nice: not exactly handsome, but quite charming, for all that."

The good lady, of course, suspected nothing; but when the King handed her his postcards, it goes without saying that she at once read the superscriptions and saw that they were addressed to the Queen Mother at San Sebastian, to the Infanta Doña Paz, to the Infanta Maria Theresa, to the prime minister.

"Why, it's the King himself!" she exclaimed, quite overcome.

Alfonso XIII was already far on his road.

The most amusing adventure, however, was that which he had at Dax. One morning, he took it into his head to motor away to the parched and desolate country of the Landes, which stretch from Bayonne to Bordeaux. After a long and wearing drive, he decided to take the train back from Dax. Accompanied by his friend Señor Quiñones de Leon, he made for the station, where the two young men, tired out and soaked in perspiration, sat down in the refreshment-room.

"Give us some lunch, please," said the King, who was ravenously hungry, to the woman at the bar.

The refreshment-room, unfortunately, was very meagerly supplied. When the two travelling-companions had eaten up the sorry fare represented by a few eggs and sandwiches, which had probably been waiting more than a month for a traveller to arrive and take a fancy to them, the King, whose appetite was far from being satisfied, called the barmaid, a fat and matronly Béarnaise, with an upper lip adorned with a pair of thick moustachios.

"Have you nothing else to give us?" he asked.

"I have a *pâté de foie gras*, but it's very expensive," said the decent creature, whose perspicacity did not go to the length of seeing a serious customer in this famished and dusty young man.

"Never mind, let's have it," said the King.

The woman brought her *pâté*, which was none too fresh; but how great was her amazement when she saw the two travellers devour not only the liver, but the fat as well! The pot was emptied and scraped clean in the twinkling of an eye.

Pleased with her successful morning's trade and encouraged by the King's ebullient good-humour, the barmaid sat down at the royal table, and began to tell the King her family affairs and questioned him with maternal solicitude. When, at last, the hour of departure struck, they shook hands with each other warmly.

Some time afterwards, the King was passing through Dax by rail and, as the train steamed into the station, said to me:

"I have an acquaintance at Dax. I'll show her to you: she is charming."

The plump Béarnaise was there, more moustachioed than ever. I will not attempt to describe her comic bewilderment at recognising her former customer in the person of the King. He was delighted and, giving her his hand:

"You won't refuse to say How-do-you-do to me, I hope?" he asked, laughing.

The thing turned her head; what was bound to happen happened: she became indiscreet. From that time onwards, she looked into every train that stopped at Dax, to see if "her friend" the King was among the passengers; and, when, instead of stepping out on the platform, he satisfied himself with giving her a friendly nod from behind the pane, she felt immensely disappointed: in fact, she was even a little offended.

The Cambo post-mistress and the Dax barmaid are not the only people who boast of having been taken in by Alfonso XIII. His turn for waggery was sometimes vented upon grave and serious men. Dr. Moure, of Bordeaux, who attended the young monarch when his nose was operated upon, has a story to tell. He was sent for, one day, to San Sebastian and was waiting for his illustrious patient in a room at the Miramar Palace, when the door opened quickly and there entered a most respectable lady, dressed in silk flounces and wearing a wig and spectacles. Not having the honour of her acquaintance, he made a deep bow, to which she replied with a stately courtesy.

"It must be the *camerera-major*," he thought to himself. "She looks tremendously eighteenth-century."

But suddenly a great burst of laughter shook the venerable dowager's frame from head to foot, her spectacles fell from her nose, her wig dropped likewise and a clarion voice cried:

"Good-morning, doctor! It's I!"

It was the King.

The chapter of anecdotes is inexhaustible. And it is not difficult to picture how this playful simplicity, combined with a delicacy of feeling and a knightly grace to which, in our age of brutal realism, we are no longer accustomed, made an utter conquest of the pretty English princess. When, after several days of familiar and daily intimacy, it became necessary to say good-bye—the princess was returning to England to busy herself with preparations for her marriage, Alfonso to Madrid for the same reason—when the moment of separation had come, there was a pang at the heart on both sides. And, as I was leaving with the princess for Paris:

"You're a lucky man, M. Paoli, to be going with the princess," said the King, sadly, as I was stepping into the railway-carriage. "I'd give anything to be in your place!"

While the Court of Spain was employed in settling, down to the smallest particular, the ceremonial for the King's approaching wedding, Princess Ena was absorbed, at one and the same time, in the charming details of her trousseau and in the more austere preparations for her conversion to Catholicism. This conversion, as I have already said, was a *sine quâ non* to the consent of Spain to her marriage.

The princess and her mother, accompanied by Miss Cochrane and Lord William Cecil, went and stayed in an hotel at Versailles for the period of religious instruction which precedes the admission of a neophyte within the pale of the Roman Catholic Church; and it was at Versailles, on a cold February morning, that she abjured her Protestantism in a sequestered chapel of the cathedral. Why did she select the town of Louis XIV in which to accomplish this important and solemn act of her life? Doubtless, because of the peaceful silence that surrounded it and of the past, filled with melancholy grandeur, which it conjured up; perhaps, also, because of the association of ideas suggested to her mind by the city of the Great King and the origins of the family of the Spanish Bourbons of which it was the cradle. The heart of woman sometimes provides instances of this delicacy of thought.

The last months of the winter of 1906 were spent by the engaged pair in eager expectation of the great event that was to unite them for good and all and in the manifold occupations which it involved. The date of the wedding was fixed for the 31st of May. A few days before that I went to Calais to meet the princess. It was as though nature, in her charming vernal awakening, was smiling upon the royal bride and had hastily decked herself in her best to greet the young princess, as she passed, with all her youthful gladness. But the princess saw nothing: she had bidden a last farewell to her country, her family and her home; and, despite the happiness that called her, the fond memory of all that she was quitting oppressed her heart.

"It is nothing, M. Paoli," she said, when I asked the cause of her sadness, "it is nothing: I cannot help feeling touched when I think that I am leaving the country where I have spent so many happy days to go towards the unknown."

She did not sleep that night. At three o'clock in the morning, she was up and dressed, ready to appear before her future husband, before the nation that was waiting to welcome her, while the King, at the same hour, was striding up and down the platform at Irun, in a fever of excitement, peering into the night so as to be the first to see the yellow gleams of the train and nervously lighting cigarette upon cigarette to calm his impatience.

Then came the whirlwind of festivals at which the King invited me to be present, the sumptuous magnificence of the marriage-ceremony in the ancient church of Los Geronimos. It was as though the old Court of Spain had regained its pomp of the days of long ago. Once more, the streets, all dressed with flags, were filled with antiquated chariots, with heraldic costumes, with glittering uniforms; from the balconies draped with precious stuffs, flowers fell in torrents; cheers rose from the serried ranks of the crowd; an intense, noisy, mad gaiety reigned in all men's eyes, on all men's lips, while, from behind the windows of the state-coach that carried her to the church, the surprised and delighted princess, forgetting her fleeting melancholy, now smiled her acknowledgments of this mighty welcome.

A tragic incident was fated brutally to interrupt her fair young dream. Finding no seat in the church of Los Geronimos, the dimensions of which are quite small, I took refuge in one of the Court stands erected along the route taken by the sovereigns; and I was watching the procession pass on its return to the palace, when my ears were suddenly deafened by a tremendous explosion. At first, no one realised where it came from. We thought that it was the report of a cannon-shot fired to announce the end of the ceremony. But suddenly loud yells arose, people hustled one another and rushed away madly, shouting:

"It's a murder! The King and Queen are killed!"

Terrified, I tried to hasten to the street from which the cries came. A file of soldiers, drawn up across the roadway stopped me. I then ran to the palace, where I arrived at exactly the same moment as the royal coach, from which the King and the young Queen alighted. They were pale, but calm. The King held his wife's hand tenderly in his own and stared in dismay at the long white train of her bridal dress, stained with great blotches of blood. Filled with horror, I went up to Alfonso XIII:

"Oh, Sir!" I cried, "at least both of you are safe and sound!"

"Yes," he replied. Then, lowering his voice, he added, "But there are some killed. Poor people! What an infamous thing!"

Under her great white veil, the Queen, standing between Queen Maria Christina and Princess Henry of Battenberg, still both trembling, wept silent tears. Then the King, profoundly moved, drew nearer to her and kissed her slowly on the cheek, whispering these charming words:

"I do hope that you are not angry with me for the emotion which I have involuntarily caused you?"

What she replied I did not hear: I only saw a kiss.

Notwithstanding the warm manifestations of loyalty which the people of Spain lavished upon their sovereigns on the following day, Queen Victoria is said to have been long haunted by the horrible spectacle which she had beheld and to have retained an intense feeling of terror and sadness from that tragic hour. But, God be praised, everything passes. When, later, I had the honour of again finding myself in attendance upon the King and Queen at Biarritz and in Paris, I recognised once more the happy and loving young couple whom I had known at the time of their engagement. Alfonso XIII had the same gaiety, the same high spirits as before; and the Queen's mind seemed to show no trace of painful memories or gloomy apprehensions.

In the course of the first journey which I took with them a year after the murderous attempt in Madrid, the King himself acquainted me with the real cause of this happy quietude so promptly recovered. Walking into the compartment where I was sitting, he lifted high into the air a pink and chubby child and, holding it up for me to look at, said, with more than a touch of pride in his voice:

"There! What do you think of him? Isn't he splendid?"

III

THE SHAH OF PERSIA

1.

Must I confess it? When I was told, a few weeks before the opening of the International Exhibition of 1900, that I should have the honour of being attached to the person of Muzaffr-ed-Din, King of Kings and Shah of Persia, during the whole duration of the official visit which he contemplated paying to Paris, I did not welcome the news with the alacrity which it ought doubtless to have evoked.

And yet I had no reason for any prejudice against this monarch: I did not even know him. My apprehensions were grounded on more remote causes: I recalled the memories which a former Shah, his predecessor, had left among us. Nasr-ed-Din was a strange and capricious sovereign, who had never succeeded in making up his mind, when he came to Europe, to leave on the further shore, so to speak, the manners and customs of his country or to lay aside the troublesome fancies in which his reckless despotism loved to indulge. Was it not related of him that, while staying in the country, in France, he caused a sheep or two to be sacrificed every morning in his bed-room, in order to ensure the Prophet's clemency until the evening? And that he had the amiable habit of buying anything that took his fancy, but neglecting to pay the bill?

Lastly, this very delicious story was told about him. The Shah had asked whether he could not, by way of amusement, be present at an execution of capital punishment during one of his stays in Paris. It so happened that the occasion offered. He was invited to go one morning to the Place de la Roquette, where the scaffold had been erected. He arrived with his diamonds and his suite; but, the moment he saw the condemned man, his generous heart was filled with a sudden tenderness for the murderer:

"Not that one. The other!" he ordered, pointing to the public prosecutor, who was presiding over the ceremony.

Picture the magistrate's face, while the Shah insisted and thought it discourteous of them not at once to yield to his wishes.

I therefore asked myself with a certain dismay what unpleasant surprises his successor might have in store for me. He seemed to me to come from the depths of a very old and mysterious form of humanity, travelling from his capital to the shores of Europe, slowly, by easy stages, as in the mediæval times, across deserts and mountains and blue-domed dead cities, escorted by a fabulous baggage-train of rare stuffs, of praying-carpets, of marvellous jewels, an army of turbaned horsemen, a swarm of officials, a harem of dancing-girls and a long file of camels.

I asked myself if I too would be obliged to assist at sacrifices of heifers and to console unpaid tradesmen, all to be finally pointed out by His Majesty as a "substitute" under the knife of the guillotine.

However, I was needlessly alarmed: in Persia, thank goodness, the Shahs succeed, but do not resemble one another. I became fully aware of this when I was admitted into the intimacy of our new guest. Muzaffr-ed-Din had nothing in common with his father. He was an overgrown child, whose massive stature, great bushy moustache, very kind, round eyes, prominent stomach and general adiposity formed a contrast with his backward mental condition and his sleepy intelligence. He had, in fact, the brain of a twelve-year-old schoolboy, together with a schoolboy's easy astonishment, candour and curiosity. He busied himself exclusively with small things, the only things that excited and interested him. He was gentle, good-natured, an arrant coward, generous at times and extremely capricious, but his whims never went so far as to take pleasure in the suffering of others. He loved life, was enormously attached to it, in fact; and he liked me too with a real affection, which was spontaneous and, at times, touching:

"Paoli, worthy Paoli," he said to me one day, in an expansive mood, fixing his round pupils upon me, "you ... my good, my dear domestic!"

When I appeared surprised and even a little offended at the place which he was allotting me in the social scale:

"His Majesty means to say," explained the grand vizier, "that he looks upon you as belonging to the family. 'Domestic' in his mind means a friend of the house, according to the true etymology of the word, which is derived from the Latin *domus*...."

The intention was pretty enough; I asked no more, remembering that Muzaffr-ed-Din spoke French with difficulty and employed a sort of negro chatter to express his thoughts.

2.

At the time of his first stay in Paris, he had the privilege of inaugurating the famous Sovereigns' Palace, which the government had fitted up in the Avenue du Bois de Boulogne for the entertainment of its royal visitors. The house was a comparatively small one; on the other hand, it was sumptuously decorated. The national furniture-repository had sent some of the finest pieces to be found in its historic store-rooms. In fact, I believe that the Shah slept in the bed of Napoleon I and washed his hands and face in the Empress Marie-Louise's basin; things that interested him but little. Great memories were a matter of indifference to him; he infinitely preferred futile realities in the form of useless objects, whose glitter pleased his eye, and of more or less harmonious sounds, whose vibrations tickled his ears.

His tastes were proved on the day of his arrival by two quick decisions: he ordered to be packed up for Teheran the grand piano which adorned his drawing-room and the motor-car which awaited his good pleasure outside, after hearing the one, trying the other and lavishly paying for both. He would not be denied.

His amazement was great when he visited the exhibition for the first time. The wonderful cosmopolitan city that seemed to have leapt into existence in the space of one of the thousand and one nights of the Persian legend stirred his eastern imagination, strive though he might to conceal the fact. The splendour of the exotic display exercised an irresistible attraction upon him; the glass-cases of jewellery also fascinated his gaze, although he himself, doubtless without realising it, was a perambulating shop-window which any jeweller might have longed to possess. On his long Persian tunic with its red edges and ample skirts creased with folds he wore a regular display of precious stones and one did not know which to admire the most, the gleaming sapphires that adorned his shoulder-straps, the splendid emeralds, the exquisite turquoises that studded the baldrick and the gold scabbard of his sword, the four enormous rubies that took the place of the buttons of his uniform, or the dazzling and formidable diamond, the famous Daria-Nour, the Sea of Light, fastened on to his *Khola*, the traditional head-dress, whence jutted like a fountain of light a quivering aigrette in brilliants. Thus decked out, Muzaffr-ed-Din was valued at thirty-four million francs net; and even then he was far from carrying the whole of his fortune upon his person: I have in fact been assured that, in the depths of the iron trunk of which four vigilant Persians had the keeping, there slumbered an equal number of precious stones, no less fine than the others and content to undergo the rigour of a temporary disgrace. At all events, in the guise in which he showed himself in public, he was enough to excite the admiring curiosity of the crowds.

In his solemn walks through the various sections of the exhibition, where my modest frock-coat looked drab and out of place among the glittering uniforms, he was attended by the grand vizier, the only dignitary entitled, by the etiquette of the Persian court, to carry a cane in the presence of his sovereign, who himself always leant upon a stick made of some precious wood. He was invariably followed by a grave and attentive Persian carrying a hand-bag. This person puzzled me at first. His fellow-countrymen treated him with respect and addressed him in deferential tones. I had concluded from this that he filled some lofty function or other and felt the more justified in so thinking as the Shah from time to time made him a little sign, whereupon, promptly, all three—the Shah, the Persian and the hand-bag—disappeared for a few moments into a dark corner. However, I soon learnt that these mysterious meetings had no political significance: the Persian was merely a confidential body-servant; as for the hand-bag, it held simply the most homely and the most intimate of all the world's utensils and the Shah was frequently obliged to have recourse to it. This little drawback, however, did not damp his eagerness to know, to see and to buy things. He bought everything indifferently: musical instruments, old tapestries, a set of table-cutlery, a panorama, a "new-art" ring, a case of pistols. He looked, touched, weighed the thing in his hand and then, raising his forefinger, said, "*Je prends*," while the delighted exhibitor, greatly touched and impressed, took down the order and the address.

Nevertheless, Muzaffr-ed-Din was not so rich as one would be inclined to think. Each time, in fact, that he came to Europe, where he spent fabulous sums, he procured the money needed for his journey, not only by raising a loan, generally in Russia, but also by a method which was both ingenious and businesslike. Before leaving his possessions, he summoned his chief officers of State—ministers, provincial governors and the like—and proposed the following bargain to them: those who wished to form part of his suite must first pay him a sum of money which he valued in accordance with the importance of their functions. It varied between 50,000 and 300,000 francs. In return, he authorised them to recoup themselves for this advance in any way they pleased. Here we find the explanation of the large number of persons who accompanied the Shah on his travels and the quaint and unexpected titles which they bore, such as that of "minister of the dockyard," though Persia has never owned a navy, and one still more extraordinary, that of "attorney to the heir apparent." Although they sometimes had romantic souls, they invariably had terribly practical minds. Eager to recover as quickly as possible the outlay to which their ambition to behold the West had induced them to consent, they practised on a huge scale and without scruple or hesitation what I may describe as the bonus or commission system. Notwithstanding my long experience of human frailties, I confess that this proceeding, cynically raised by these gentlemen to the level of an institution, upset all my notions, while it explained how the Shah was able to spend eight to twelve million francs in pocket-money on each of his trips to France.

As soon as the people about him knew what shops His Majesty proposed to visit in the course of his daily drive, a bevy of courtiers would swoop down upon the awestruck tradesman and imperiously insist upon his promising them a big commission, in exchange for which they undertook to prevail upon His Majesty graciously to honour the establishment with his custom. The shopkeeper as a rule raised no objection; he was quite content to increase the price in proportion; and, when the good Shah, accompanied by his vizier and the famous hand-bag, presented himself a few hours later in the shop, his suite praised the goods of the house so heartily that he never failed to let fall the traditional phrase, "*Je prends*," so as to give no one even the slightest pain. Nor, for that matter, did any of those who surrounded him dream of making a secret of the traffic in which he indulged behind his sovereign's back: it was a right duly acquired and paid for.

I am bound to say, however, that the grand vizier—no doubt because he was already too well-off—appeared to be above these sordid and venial considerations. This important personage, whose name on that occasion was His Highness the Sadrazani Mirza Ali Asghar Khan Emin es Sultan, combined an acute understanding with a superior cast of mind; the Shah showed him a very noteworthy affection and treated him as a friend. These marks of special kindness were due to curious causes, which an amiable Persian was good enough to reveal to me. It appears that, when the late Shah Nasr-ed-Din was shot dead at the mosque where he was making a pilgrimage, the grand vizier of the time, who was none other than this same Mirza Ali Asghar Khan, pretended that the Shah's wound was not serious, had the corpse seated in the carriage and drove back to the palace beside it, acting as if he were talking to his sovereign, fanning him and asking occasionally for water to quench his thirst, as though he were still alive.

The death was not acknowledged till some days later. In this way, the vizier gave the heir-apparent, the present Shah, time to return from Tanris and avoided the grave troubles that would certainly have arisen had the truth been known. Muzaffr-ed-Din owned his crown and perhaps his life to his grand vizier; small wonder that he showed him some gratitude.

His court minister, Mohamed Khan, could also have laid claim to this gratitude, for he gave proof of remarkable presence of mind at the time of the attempted assassination of which Muzaffr-ed-Din was the object during his stay in Paris in 1900.

The incident is perhaps still in the reader's recollection. The Shah, with the court minister by his side and General Parent, the chief French officer attached to his person, seated facing him, had just left the Sovereign's Palace to drive to the exhibition, when a man sprang on the step of the open landau, produced a revolver and took aim at the monarch's chest. Before he had time, however, to pull the trigger, a hand of iron fell upon his wrist and clutched it with such force that the man was compelled to let go his revolver, which fell at the feet of the sovereign, while the would-be murderer was arrested by the police. Mohamed Khan, by this opportune and energetic interference, had prevented a shot the consequences of which would have been disastrous for the Shah and very annoying for the French government, all the more so inasmuch as the author of this attempt was a French subject, a sort of fanatic from the South, to whom the recent assassination of King Humbert of Italy had suggested this fantastic plan of making away with the unoffending Muzaffr-ed-Din. Here is a curious detail: I had received that very morning an anonymous letter, dated from Naples, but posted in Paris, in which the sovereign was warned that an attempt would be made on his life. Although this kind of communication was frequent, I had ordered the supervision to be redoubled inside the palace; as a matter of fact, I did not much fear a surprise outside, as the Shah never drove out but his carriage was surrounded by a detachment of cavalry. Now ill-luck would have it that he took it into his head to go out that day before the time which he himself had fixed and without waiting for the arrival of the escort: I have shown the result.

During the whole of this tragic scene, which lasted only a few seconds, he did not utter a single word; the pallor which had overspread his cheeks alone betrayed the emotion which he had felt. Nevertheless, he ordered the coachman to drive on. When, at last, they reached the Champs Élysées and he perceived numerous groups waiting to cheer him, he emerged from his stupor:

"Is it going to begin again?" he cried, in accents of terror.

3.

He was given, in fact, to easy and strange fits of alarm. He always carried a loaded pistol in his trowsers-pocket, though he never used it. On one of his journeys in France, he even took it into his head to make a high court-official walk before him when he left the theatre, carrying a revolver pointed at the peaceable sightseers who had gathered to see him come out. As soon as I saw this, I ran up to the threatening body-guard:

"Put that revolver away," I said. "It's not the custom here."

But I had to insist pretty roughly before he consented to put away his weapon.

The Shah, for that matter, was no less distrustfull of his own subjects; in fact, I observed that, when the Persians were in his presence, they adopted a uniform attitude which consisted in holding their hands crossed on their stomach, no doubt as evidence of their harmless intentions. It was a guarantee of a very casual sort, we must admit.

For the rest, his "alarms" displayed themselves under the most diverse aspects and in the most unexpected circumstances. For instance, there was no persuading him ever to ascend the Eiffel Tower. The disappointment of his guides was increased by the fact that he would come as far as the foot of the pillars; they always thought that he meant to go up. But no: once below the immense iron framework, he gazed up in the air, examined the lifts, flung a timid glance at the staircases, then suddenly turned on his heels and walked away. They told him in vain that his august father had gone up as far as the first floor; nothing could induce him to do as much.

I again remember a day—it was at the time of his second stay in Paris—when, on entering his drawing-room, I found him wearing a very careworn air.

"Paoli," he said, taking my hand and leading me to the window, "look!"

Look as I might, I saw nothing out of the way. Down below, three bricklayers stood on the pavement, talking quietly together.

"What!" said the Shah. "Don't you see those men standing still, down there. They have been there for an hour, talking and watching my window. Paoli, they want to kill me."

Repressing a terrible wish to laugh, I resolved to reassure our guest with a lie:

"Why, I know them!" I replied. "I know their names: they are decent working-men."

Muzaffr-ed-Din's face lit up at once:

"You seem to know everybody," he said, giving me a grateful look.

THE SHAH OF PERSIA

The most amusing incident was that which happened on the occasion of an experiment with radium. I had described to the sovereign, in the course of conversation, the wonderful discovery which our great *savant*, M. Currie, had just made, a discovery that was called upon to revolutionise science. The Shah was extremely interested by my story and repeatedly expressed a desire to be shown the precious magic stone. Professor Currie was informed accordingly, and, in spite of his stress of work, agreed to come to the Élysée Palace Hôtel and give an exhibition. As, however, complete darkness was needed for radium to be admired in all its brilliancy, I had with endless trouble persuaded the King of Kings to come down to one of the hotel cellars arranged for the purpose. At the appointed time, His Majesty and all his suite proceeded to the underground apartment in question. Professor Currie closed the door, switched off the electric light and uncovered his specimen of radium, when, suddenly, a shout of terror, resembling at one and the same time the roar of a bull and the yells of a man who is being murdered, rang out, followed by hundreds of similar cries. Amid general excitement and consternation, we flung ourselves upon the electric switches, turned on the lights and beheld a strange sight: in the midst of the prostrate Persians stood the Shah, his arms clinging to the neck of his howling grand vizier, his round pupils dilated to their rims, while he shouted at the top of his voice, in Persian:

"Come away! Come away!"

The switching on of the light calmed this mad anguish as though by magic. Realising the disappointment which he had caused M. Currie, he tried to offer him a decoration by way of compensation; but the austere man of science thought right to decline it.

The instinctive dread of darkness and solitude was so keen in the Persian monarch that he required his bed-room to be filled during the night with light and sound. Accordingly, every evening, as soon as he had lain down and closed his eyes, the members of his suite gathered round his bed, lit all the candelabra and exchanged their impressions aloud, while young nobles of the court, relieving one another in pairs, conscientiously patted his arms and legs with little light, sharp, regular taps. The King of Kings imagined that he was in this way keeping death at a distance, if perchance it should take a fancy to visit him in his sleep, and the extraordinary thing is that he did sleep, notwithstanding all this massage, light and noise.

4.

The need which he felt of having people constantly around him and of reproducing the atmosphere of his distant country wherever he fixed his temporary residence was reflected in the picturesque and singularly animated aspect which the hotel or palace at which he elected to stay assumed soon after his installation. It was promptly transformed into a vast, exotic caravanserai, presenting the appearance of a French fair combined with that of an eastern bazaar. The house was taken possession of by its new occupants from the kitchens, ruled over by the Persian master-cook who prepared the monarch's dishes, to the attics, where the inferior servants were accommodated. One saw nothing but figures in dark tunics and astrakhan caps, squatting in the passages, leaning over the staircases; along the corridors and in the halls, the shopkeepers had improvised stalls as at Teheran, in the hope that the monarch would let fall from his august lips in passing the "*Je prends*" that promised wealth. In the uncouth crowd which the desire of provoking and hearing that blessed phrase attracted to the waiting-rooms of the hotel, all the professions rubbed shoulders promiscuously; curiosity-dealers, unsuccessful inventors, collectors of autographs and postage-stamps, ruined financiers, charlatans, unknown artists, women of doubtful character.

Their numbers had increased so greatly, on the faith of the legend that the Shah's treasures were inexhaustible, that a radical step had to be taken: when Muzaffr-ed-Din returned to Paris in 1902 and 1905, the applicants for favours were forbidden to resume their little manœuvre. Thereupon they changed their tactics: they sat down and wrote.

I have kept these letters, which the Shah never read and which his secretary handed me regularly, without having read them either. They arrived by each post in shoals. One could easily make a volume of them which would provide psychologists with a very curious study of the human soul and mind. Among those poor letters are many obscure, touching, comic, candid and cynical specimens; some also are absurd; others imprudent or sad. Most of them are signed; and among the signatures of these requests for assistance are names which one is surprised to find there. I must be permitted to suppress these names and to limit myself, in this mad orgie of epistolary literature, to reproducing the most typical of the letters that fell under my eyes.

First, a few specimens of "the comic note:"

"*To His Majesty, Muzaffr-ed-Din, Shah of Persia.* "Your Majesty,—

"Knowing that you look kindly upon French requests, I venture to address these few lines to you. I am expecting my sister, Mlle. Crampel, who has a situation in Russia; as she is ill, I would like her to remain in France. For us to live together, I should have to start a business with a capital of 3 to 5,000 francs, which I do not possess and which I cannot possibly find. I am 58 years of age.

"In the hope that you will lend a favourable ear to my request, I am

"Your Majesty's most humble servant,

"MADAME M.

"P. S.—In gratitude, with Your Majesty's permission, I would place a sign representing Your Majesty over the shop-front."

"*Sire,*—

"The feeling that prompts me to write to you, O noble King, is the love which I feel for your country. I will come straight to the point: I will ask you, O Majesty, if I, a plain French subject, may have a post of some kind in your ideal kingdom.

"Dentist I am; a dentist I would remain, in Your Majesty's service. All my life long, you would be assured of my complete devotion.

"A future Persian dentist to his future King.

"P. J. L.

"Pray, Sire, address the reply to the *poste restante* at Post-office No. 54."

"*Great Shah,*—

"This missive which I have the honour of addressing to Your Majesty is to tell you that I and my friends, Messieurs Jules Brunel and Abel Chenet, have the honour of offering you four bottles of champagne and two bottles of claret.

"In exchange, may we beg for the Order of the Lion and Sun, which it would give us great pleasure to receive and which we hope that Your Majesty will confer upon us? We are French citizens and old soldiers.

"We wish you constant good health and prosperity for your country, Persia. You can send your servant to fetch the bottles.

"We have the honour to greet you and we remain your very humble servants, crying:

"'Long live H. M. Muzaffr-ed-Din and long live Persia!'

"A. W."

"THORIGNY (ON MY WAY HOME),

"27 August, 1902.

"*Your Majesty,*—

"Yesterday, Tuesday, I was in Paris, waiting to have the pleasure of seeing you leave your hotel. That pleasure was not vouchsafed me.

"But, on the other hand, a ring set with a diamond, which I was taking to be repaired, was stolen from me by a pickpocket.

"This ring was the only diamond which my wife possessed. In consequence of the theft, she now possesses none.

"I put myself the question whether I could not indict you before a French court, as being the direct cause of the theft.

"I find nothing in our French law-books likely to decide in my favour.

"And so I prefer to come and beseech you to redress the involuntary injury which you have done me.

"A choice stone, which I could have set as a ring, would make good all the damage which I have suffered.

"I am well aware that you must have numerous and various requests for assistance. This is not one of them.

"But I should be infinitely grateful to you if you would understand that, but for your coming to Paris, I should not have been robbed and if you would kindly send me a choice stone to replace the one stolen from me.

"Will Your Majesty pray receive the homage of my most profound respect.

"G. P.

"*Attorney-at-law*,

"BARBEZIEUX (Gironde), France."

"*To His Majesty*,—

"*Muzaffr-ed-Din, Shah of Persia,*

"*At the Élysée Palace Hôtel, Paris.*

"I eagerly congratulate His Majesty on the great honour which he has paid the French people by making a long stay in the great international city. And I take advantage of this occasion to beg His Majesty to initiate a general convocation of all the sovereigns of the whole world for next month, in order to open a subscription for the construction of an unprecedented fairy palace (new style and taking something from planetary nature and its marvels), to be known as the Sovereign Palace of the Universal Social Congress, symbolising the whole universe by States, containing the apartments of every sovereign in the world and situated near the Bois de Boulogne.

"I consider that His Majesty would thus have a good opportunity of securing a great page in history.

"Hoping for a just appreciation and entire success, I send His Majesty, the Shah of Persia, the assurance of my greatest respect, together with my perfect consideration, and I am,

"The most humble Architect-general of the Universal Confederation of Social Peace,

"At His Majesty's service,

"C. M."

Now comes the touching note:

"A little provincial work-girl, who has not the honour of being known to His Majesty, kneels down before him and, with her hands folded together, entreats him to make her a present of a sum of 1,200 francs, which would enable her to marry the young man she loves.... Oh, what blessings he would receive day by day for that kind action!

"I beg the Shah to forgive me for the offences of this letter against etiquette, with which I am not acquainted. I kiss His Majesty's hands and I am

"His most humble and obedient little servant,

"A. C."

Lastly, is not the following letter an exquisitely candid specimen of the proper art of "sponging"?

"Your Majesty,—

"As you are a friend of France, I propose to write to you as a friend; you will permit me to do so, I hope.

"The question is this: I have the greatest longing to set eyes on the sea; my husband has a few days' holiday in the course of October; I should like to make the most of it and to go away for a little while.

"Our means are very small indeed; my husband has only 105 francs a month; and I could not do what I wish without encroaching on my housekeeping money, which is calculated down to the last centime.

"I therefore remembered your generosity and thought that you might be touched by my request.

"You would not like a little Paris woman to be prevented from enjoying the sight of the sea which you have doubtless often admired.

"You are very fond of travelling; you will understand my curiosity.

"Will Your Majesty deign to accept the expression of my most respectful and distinguished sentiments?

"MME. A. A."

A worthy woman sent this rich note:

"*To His Majesty, the King of Persia,*—

"My name is the Widow Bressoy, aged 82. I have lost my husband and two of my daughters; I am unable to walk and I owe a quarter's rent. My grandmother washed for His Majesty King Louis-Philippe of France; H. R. H. the Duc d' Aumale used to help me with my rent; show your kind heart and do as he did. Should you come to the church of Ste. Elisabeth du Temple on Sunday next, I should be very glad to see you.

"I am

"Your Majesty's most respectful servant,

"WIDOW BRESSOY."

The following original proposal came from a well-known business-house:

"*Sir,*—

"After the Monza crime and the attempt of which you were the object yesterday and in view of the solemnities during which you might be too much exposed to danger, I consider it my duty to bring to your notice certain particulars which might be of the greatest use to you and those about your person.

"I refer to secret waistcoats of my own manufacture which I am able to offer to you and which are absolutely warranted.

"The waistcoat which I am offering is proof against a revolver-bullet and, of course, against a sword or dagger.

"As an absolute guarantee, I can assure you as follows by experiment: the fabric consists of a very close and solidly-riveted coat of steel mail; the shape of the links has been specially studied so as to allow of great suppleness, while preserving the greatest solidity.

"It resists the 12 *mm.* bullet of the regulation revolver, 1874 pattern.

"I have specimens at which bullets were fired at a distance of 4 yards; they give an exact idea of the resisting power.

"The coat of mail is lined with silk or satin, which gives the appearance of an ordinary garment and does not for a moment suggest its special object.

"The waistcoat covers and protects the back, the chest, the stomach and is continued down the abdomen.

"I must add that the waistcoat is very easy to wear and in no way inconvenient, on condition that I am supplied with the necessary measurements or, better still, with an ordinary day-waistcoat of the wearer's, fitted to his size.

"Hoping in the circumstances to be of some use to you, I beg Your Majesty to accept the expression of my most profound respect.

"R. G."

Let us pass to the children. Less unreasonable than their parents, they content themselves with asking for postage-stamps, bicycles or autographs.

First comes a public schoolboy, quite proud of incidentally showing that he knows his classics:

"*Sire,—*

"When you first set foot on French soil, you were pleased to take notice, at Maubeuge railway-station, of a young public schoolboy, who, not knowing your quality, was only able to give you a very respectful greeting. That young schoolboy was myself.

"I realised the extent of the signal honour which Your Majesty did me when I learnt that I had received it from the sovereign of Persia, the country of Xerxes and Darius, the land whose children have filled the world with the fame of their exploits. And, descending the course of the ages, reverting to the lessons of my masters, I hailed in you 'the wise and enlightened monarch whose reign opens out so many hopes.'

"Sire, I shall never forget that moment, which will probably be the only one of its kind in my life; but, if I were permitted to express a desire, I would humbly confess to Your Majesty that my greatest happiness would be to possess a collection of Persian postage-stamps, as an official token of the honour which you condescended to do me.

"Deign, Sire, etc.

"R. W.

"*Pupil at The Lycée Faidherbe, Lille*

"(on my holidays)."

The next has not yet learnt the beauties of literary style; he has less notions of form; but his ambition is more far-reaching:

"*Your Majesty,*—

"I begin by begging your pardon for my presumption; but I have heard everybody say and I read in the paper that Your Majesty is greatly interested in motor-cars. I therefore thought that you must also have ridden the bicycle, which you now, no doubt, care less for; and it occurred to me that, if you happened to have an old one put by, Your Majesty might do me the honour to give it to me.

"Papa and my big brother Jean go out riding on their bicycles and I am left at home with mamma, because I have not a machine and they cannot afford to buy me one.

"I should be so proud to have a bicycle, given me by Your Majesty.

"I shall not tell papa that I am writing to Your Majesty, because he would laugh at me, and I shall take three sous from my purse for the stamp on this letter.

"I pray God not to let those wicked anarchists attack Your Majesty, to whom I offer my profound respect.

"MAURICE LELANDAIS,

"*aged 9½ years,*

"living with his family, *Faubourg Bizienne,*

"GUÉRANDE (*Loire-Inférieure*)."

Another schoolboy:

"VERVIERS, 3 September.

"*Great King of Persia in France, Sir,*—

"I have read in the paper that you are very rich and have lots of gold.

"My father promised to give me a gold watch for my first communion next year, if I worked hard at school.

"I did study, Sir, for I was second and the first is thirteen years old and I am only eleven and a half. To prove it to you, here is my prize-list. Now, when I ask if I shall have my watch, my father answers that he has no money and he wants it all for bread. It is not right, Sir, to deceive me like that. But I hope that you will give me what they refuse. Do me that great pleasure. I will pray for you.

"I love you very much.

"M. J."

Here is an artless request from a little English girl:

"*Your Majesty,*—

"I hear you are taking a holiday in Paris and I think that this must be the best time to write to you, for you will not be so busy as in your own kingdom.

"First of all, I want to tell you that I am an English girl, fourteen years of age, and my name is Mary. I love collecting autographs and so far I have been very lucky and have got some of celebrities, but I have none of a King, except Menelik, who is a black majesty.

"Now I should ever so much like to have a few lines in your handwriting.

"Do be so very kind as to write to me.

"MARY ST. J."

To conclude with, here are a few lively letters from ladies dark and fair:

"PARIS, 27 July.

"*Sir,*—

"I won the last beauty-prize at Marienbad and I am simply dying to make your acquaintance.

"In this hope, I have the honour to greet you.

"FERNANDE DE B."

"MARSEILLES, 1 August.

"*Sire,*—

"It is a pleasure to me to write to you. From my childhood's days, I have admired Persia, that beautiful country, so dear to my heart. Since I have heard you mentioned, I love you, Sire; I should like to be at your service. I do not know the Persian language, but, if you adopt me, I shall know it in a few days and you shall be my master.

"Receive, Sire, my sincere greetings.

"MIREILLE———.

"P. S.—Please reply. I will start for Paris at once."

"PARIS, 29 July.

"*To Monsieur Muzaffr-ed-Din.*

"*Monsieur Le Chah,*—

"Forgive me for taking the liberty of writing to you. I had the pleasure of seeing you yesterday in the Avenue du Bois de Boulogne and of receiving a wave of the hand from you and a most gracious smile.

"How I should love to make your acquaintance and to have the pleasure of pressing your hand!

"You may be certain of my entire discretion. You can, if you do not mind, appoint whatever time and place you please.

"I should be very happy to see you; and I may venture to add that I am a very handsome woman.

"Believe me,

"Monsieur le Chah,

"Yours most cordially,

"MADAME MARGUERITE L.

"P. S.—I beg you to destroy this letter."

"*To His Majesty, Muzaffr-ed-Din,*—

"We should be greatly honoured if you would do us the honour to come and spend a few days in the principality of Monaco.

"A group of ladies:

"BLANCHE.
"JEANNE.
"ADÈLE."

5.

All these efforts of the imagination, all these prodigies of ingenuity, all these amorous suggestions were wasted. As I have said, the Shah took no notice whatever of the six hundred and odd begging letters of different kinds addressed to him during his visits to France. Pleasure-loving and capricious, careful of his own peace of mind, he dreaded and avoided emotions. Nevertheless, he was not insensible to pity nor indifferent to the charms of the fair sex. At certain times, he was capable of sudden movements of magnificent generosity: he would readily give a diamond to some humble workwoman whom he met on his way; he would of his own accord hand a bank-note to a beggar; he freely distributed Persian gold-pieces stamped with his effigy.

He would also fall a victim to sudden erotic fancies that sometimes caused me moments of cruel embarrassment. I remember that, one afternoon, when we were driving in the Bois de Boulogne, near the lakes, Muzaffr-ed-Din noticed a view which he admired, ordered the carriages to stop and expressed a desire himself to take some snapshots of the charming spot. We at once alighted. A little further, a group of smart ladies sat chatting gaily without taking the smallest heed of our presence. The Shah, seeing them, asked me to beg them to come closer so that he might photograph them. Although I did not know them, I went upand spoke to them and, with every excuse, explained the sovereign's whim to them. Greatly amused, they yielded to it with a good grace. The Shah took the photograph, smiled to the ladies and, when the operation was over, called me to him again:

THE SHAH LEAVING THE ÉLYSEÉ PALACE FOR A WALK

"Paoli," he said, "they are very pretty, very nice; go and ask them if they would like to come back with me to Teheran."

Imagine my face! I had to employ all the resources of my eloquence to make the King of Kings understand that you cannot take a woman to Teheran, as you would a piano; a cinematograph or a motor-car, and that you cannot say of her, as of an article in a shop, "*Je prends*."

I doubt whether he really grasped the force of my arguments, for, some time after, when we were at the Opera in the box of the President of the Republic, we perceived with dismay that His Persian Majesty, instead of watching the performance on the stage—consisting of that exquisite ballet *Coppélia*, with some of our prettiest dancers taking part in it—kept his opera-glass obstinately fixed on a member of the audience in the back row of the fourth tier, giving signs of manifest excitement as he did so. I was beginning to wonder with anxiety whether he had caught sight of some "suspicious face," when the court minister, in whose ear he had whispered a few words, came over to me and said, with an air of embarrassment:

"His Majesty feels a profound admiration for a lady up there. Do you see? The fourth seat from the right. His Majesty would be obliged to you if you would enable him to make her acquaintance. You can tell her, if you like, as an inducement, that my sovereign will invite her to go back with him to Teheran."

"Again!"

Although this sort of errand did not fall within the scope of my instructions, I regarded the worthy Oriental's idea as so comical that I asked one of my detectives who, dressed to the nines, was keeping guard outside the presidential box, whether he would care to go upstairs and, if possible, convey the flattering invitation to the object of the imperial flame. My Don Juan by proxy assented and set out on his mission.

The Shah's impatience increased from moment to moment. The last act had begun when I saw my inspector return alone and looking very sheepish:

"Well," I asked, "what did she say?"

"She boxed my ears."

The sovereign, when the grand vizier conveyed this grievous news to him, knitted his bushy eyebrows, declared that he was tired, and ordered his carriage.

My duty as a conscientious historian obliges me, however, to mention the fact that Muzaffr-ed-Din did not always meet with such piteous rebuffs in the field of gallantry upon which he gladly ventured. He kept up a very fond and regular flirtation in Paris with a French favourite, a charming and exceedingly beautiful person, who had been seduced by the bejewelled opulence of the King of Kings. She had rooms in the monarch's hotel each time he came to France; and they retained a sort of affection for each other notwithstanding the mutual disappointment which they had experienced: she, because she thought that he was generous; he, because he hoped that she was disinterested. That she was anxious to turn a great man's friendship to account can, strictly speaking, be imagined; on the other hand, it is incomprehensible that the Shah, who was so easily moved to generosity towards the first comer, should display a sordid avarice towards the woman whom he himself had selected from among so many. Perhaps he was ingenuous enough to wish to be loved for his own sake. At any rate, this continual misunderstanding led to intensely funny scenes. The young woman, exasperated by obtaining nothing but promises each time she expressed the desire to possess a pearl necklace or a diamond ring, ended by resorting to heroic methods: she locked her door when the Shah announced his coming. The King of Kings stamped, threatened, implored.

"My diamonds first! My pearls first!" she replied, from behind the locked door.

In vain he offered the worn-out journey to Teheran: it was no good. Then, resigning himself, he sent for the necklace or the ring. In this way, she collected a very handsome set of jewellery.

Although, as I have said, her rooms were next to his own, Muzaffr-ed-Din saw comparatively little of her; he had not the time; his days were too full of engagements. Rising very early in the morning, he devoted long hours to his toilet, to his prayers and to his political conversations with the grand vizier. He worked as little as possible, but saw many people; he liked giving audiences to doctors and purveyors. He always had his meals alone, in accordance with Persian etiquette, and was served at one time with European dishes, which were better suited to his impaired digestive organs, and at another with Persian fare, consisting of slices of Ispahan melon, with white and flavoursome flesh; of the national dish called *pilaf tiobab*, in which meat cut up and mixed with delicate spices lay spread on a bed of rice just scalded, underdone and crisp; of hard-boiled eggs and young marrows; or else of *stilo* grill, represented by scallops of mutton soaked in aromatic vinegar and cooked over a slow fire of pinewood embers; lastly, of aubergine fritters, of which he was very fond. I am bound, for that matter, to say that Persian cooking, which I had many opportunities of tasting, is delicious and that the dishes which I have named would have done honour to any Parisian bill of fare.

After rising from table, Muzaffr-ed-Din generally devoted an hour to taking a nap, after which we went out either for a drive round the Bois or to go and see the shops or the Paris sights. To tell the truth, we hardly ever knew beforehand what the sovereign's plans were. He seemed to take a mischievous delight in altering the afternoon programme and route which I had worked out with his approval in the morning. Thanks to his whims, I lived in a constant state of alarm.

"I want to see some museums to-day," he would say at eleven o'clock. "We will start at two."

I at once informed the minister of fine-arts, who told off his officials to receive him; I telephoned to the military governor of Paris to send an escort.

At three o'clock, we were still waiting. At last, just about four, he appeared, with a look of indifference and care on his face, and told me that he would much prefer to go for a drive in the Bois de Boulogne.

One day, after he had spent the morning in listening to a chapter of the life of Napoleon I, he beckoned to me on his way to lunch.

"M. Paoli," he said, "I want to go to the Château de Fontainebleau to-day."

"Well, Sir, you see."

"Quick, quick!"

There was no arguing the matter. I rushed to the telephone, warned the panic-stricken P. L. M. Co., that we must have a special train at all costs and informed the keeper of the palace and the dumb-foundered sub-prefect of our imminent arrival at Fontainebleau.

When the Shah, still under the influence of his morning's course of reading, stepped from the carriage, two hours later, before the gate of the palace, he was seized with a strange freak: he demanded that the dragoons who had formed his escort from the station should dismount and enter the famous Cour des Adieux after him. Next he made them fall into line in the middle of the great quadrangle, leant against the steps, looked at them long and fondly, muttered a few sentences in Persian and then disappeared inside the palace.

Greatly alarmed, we thought at first that he had gone mad; at last we understood: he had been enacting the scene in which the emperor takes leave of his grenadiers. It may have been very flattering for the dragoons; I doubt if it was quite so flattering for Napoleon.

His visit to the Louvre Museum will also linger in my memory among the amusing episodes of his stay in Paris. M. Leyques, who was at that time Minister of Fine Arts and in this capacity did the honours of the museum to the Shah, had resolved carefully to avoid showing our guest the Persian room, fearing lest the King of Kings, who perhaps did not grasp the importance of the priceless collection which Mme. Dieulafoy and M. Morgan had brought back with them, should show a keen vexation at finding himself in the presence of jewels and mosaics which he might have preferred to see in his own country.

The minister, therefore, conducted him through the picture and sculpture-galleries, trying to befog his mind and tire his legs, so that he might declare his curiosity satisfied as soon as possible.

Lo and behold, however, the Shah suddenly said:

"Take me to the Persian room!"

There was no evading the command. M. Leyques, obviously worried, whispered an order to the chief attendant and suggested to the Shah that he should take a short rest before continuing his inspection. The Shah agreed.

Meantime, in the Persian room, keepers and attendants hurriedly cleared away the more valuable ornaments and mosaics, so that Muzaffr-ed-Din should not feel any too cruel regrets; and at last the King of Kings, far from revealing any disappointment, declared himself delighted to find in Paris so well-arranged a collection of curious remains of ancient Persian architecture and art. And he added, slily:

"When I have a museum at Teheran, I shall see that we have a French room."

For that matter, he was often capable of administering a sort of snub when we thought that we were providing him with a surprise. For instance, one day, when, with a certain self-conceit, I showed him our three camels in the Jardin d' Acclimatation:

"I own nine thousand!" he replied, with a scornful smile.

Our Zoological gardens did not interest him; he only really enjoyed himself there twice to my knowledge. The first time was when, at his own request, he was allowed to witness the repugnant sight of a boa-constrictor devouring a live rabbit. This produced, the next morning, the following letter from "a working milliner," which I print "with all faults:"

"*Monsieur le Chah,*—

"You have been to the Jardin d' Aclimatation (*sic*) and watched the boa-constrictor eating a live rabbit. This was very interesting, so you said. Ugh! How could the King of Kings, an excellency, a majesty, find pleasure in the awful torments of that poor rabbit? I hate people who like going to bull-fights. Cruelty and cowardice go hand in hand. Are you one of the company, monsieur le Chah?"

The second time that he seemed to amuse himself was on the occasion of a wedding-dance that was being held in a room next to that in which he had stopped to take tea. On hearing the music, he suddenly rose and opened the door leading to the ball-room. The appearance of the devil in person would not have produced a greater confusion than that of this potentate wearing his tall astrakhan cap and covered with diamonds. But he, without the least uneasiness, went the round of the couples, shook hands with the bride and bridegroom, gave them pieces of Persian gold money and made his excuses to the bride for not having a necklace about him to offer her. I was waiting for him to invite her to accompany him to Teheran; the husband's presence no doubt frightened him.

He seldom left his rooms at night. Sometimes he went to circus performances or an extravaganza or musical play; he preferred, however, to devote his evenings to more domestic enjoyments; he loved the pleasures of home life: sometimes, he played with his little sons, "the little Shahs," as they were called, nice little boys of seven to thirteen; at other times, he indulged in his favourite games, chess and billiards. He played with his grand vizier, his minister of the ceremonies or myself. The stakes were generally twenty francs, sometimes a hundred. We did our best to lose, for, if we had the bad luck to win, he would show his ill-temper by suddenly throwing up the game and retiring into a corner, where his servants lit his great Persian pipe for him, the *kaljan*, a sort of Turkish narghileh, filled with a scented tobacco called *tombeki*. Often, also, to console himself for his mortification at billiards, he called for music. I then heard songs behind the closed hangings, harsh, strange and also very sweet songs, accompanied on the piano or the violin; it was a sort of evocation of the East in a modern frame; and the contrast, I must say, was rather pleasing.

6.

The Shah and I grew accustomed to each other, little by little, and became the best of friends. He refused to go anywhere without me; I took part in the drives, in the games at billiards, in the concerts, in all the journeys. We went to Vichy, to Vittel, to Contrexéville. It was here, at Contrexéville, where he had come for the cure, that I saw him for the last time. His eccentricities, his whims and his diamonds, had produced the usual effect on the peaceful population of the town.

A few days after his arrival, hearing that H. I. H. the grand-duchess Vladimir of Russia had taken up her quarters at an hotel near his own, he hastened to call and pay his respects and departed from his habits to the length of inviting her to luncheon.

On the appointed day, the grand-duchess, alighting from her carriage before the residence of her host, found the Shah waiting for her on the threshold in a grey frock-coat with a rose in his buttonhole. He ceremoniously led her by the hand to the dining-room, making her walk through his rooms, the floors of which he had had covered with the wonderful kachan carpets that accompanied him on all his journeys. The princess, charmed with these delicate attentions on the great man's part, was beginning to congratulate herself on the pleasant surprise which Persian civilisation caused her when—we had hardly sat down to table—a chamberlain went up to the King of Kings, bowed low and handed him a gold salver on which lay a queer-looking and at first indescribable object. The Shah, without blinking, carelessly put out his hand, took the thing between his fingers and, with an easy and familiar movement, inserted it in his jaw: it was a set of false teeth. Imagine the consternation!

But it was worse still when, about the middle of the meal, the sovereign, suddenly interrupting his conversation with Her Imperial Highness, rose without a word, disappeared and returned in five minutes to resume his place with a smile, after the court minister had taken care to announce aloud that "His Majesty had had to leave the room."

The grand-duchess, as may be imagined, retained an unforgettable memory of this lunch, the more so as the Shah, perhaps in order to wipe out any unpleasant impression that might linger in her mind, did a very gallant thing; the next day, the Princess Vladimir received a bale of Persian carpets of inestimable value, accompanied by a letter from the grand vizier begging her, in the name of his sovereign, to accept this present, His Majesty having declared that he would not allow other feet to tread carpets on which Her Imperial Highness's had rested.

I, less fortunate than the grand-duchess, never, alas, succeeded in obtaining possession of the one and only carpet which Muzaffr-ed-Din had deigned—quite spontaneously—to offer me.

"My ministers will see that you get it," he said.

When the day for his departure for Persia drew near, I thought that it would be wise to ask the court minister for my carpet in my most respectful manner.

"Oh," he replied, "does it belong to you? The only thing is that it has been packed up, by mistake, with the others. If you want it, they can give it to you in the train."

As I was to accompany our guest as far as the German frontier, I waited until we had left Vichy and discreetly repeated my request at the first stop.

"Certainly," said the minister, "you shall have it at the next station."

I was beginning to feel uneasy. At the following stopping-place, there was no sign of a carpet. We were approaching the frontier, where my mission ended. I, therefore, resolved to apply to the minister of public-works.

"Your excellency."

"Your carpet?" he broke in. "Quite right, my dear M. Paoli. The orders have been given and you shall have it when you leave us at the other station."

But here again, alas, nothing! And, as I complained to a third excellency of this strange piece of neglect:

"It's an omission. Come with us as far as Strassburg, where you will receive satisfaction."

At this rate, they would have carried me, by easy stages, to Teheran. I, therefore, gave up all hopes of my carpet. And, taking leave of these amiable functionaries, I heard the good Shah's voice crying in the distance:

"Good-bye, Paoli, worthy Paoli! Till our next meeting!"

I never saw him again.

IV

THE TSAR NICHOLAS II AND THE TSARITSA ALEXANDRA FEODOROVNA

THE EMPEROR AND EMPRESS OF RUSSIA AND THE GRAND DUKE ALEXIS

1.

One morning in June, 1901, I had just reached the Ministry of the Interior and was entering my office, when a messenger came up to me and said, solemnly:

"The Prime Minister would like to speak to you at once, sir."

When a public official is sent for by his chief,[1] the first thought that flashes across his brain is that of disgrace, and he instinctively makes a rapid and silent examination of conscience to quiet his anxious mind, unless, indeed, he only ends by alarming it. Nevertheless, I admit that when I received this message, I took it philosophically. The Prime Minister, at that time, was M. Waldeck-Rousseau. It is not my business here to pass judgment on the politician; and I have retained a most pleasant recollection of the man. To attractions more purely intellectual he added a certain cordiality. He looked upon events and upon life itself from the point of view of a more or less disillusioned dilettante; and this made him at once satirical, indulgent and obliging. He honoured me with a kindly friendship, notwithstanding the fact that he used to reproach me, in his jesting way, with becoming too much of a reactionary from my contact with the monarchs of Europe and that I once took his breath away by telling him that I had dined with the Empress Eugénie at Cap Martin.

"A republican official at the Empress's table!" he cried. "You're the only man, my dear Paoli, who would dare to do such a thing. And you're the only one," he added, slily, "in whom we would stand it!"

For all that, when I entered his room on this particular morning, I was struck with his thoughtful air; and my surprise increased still further when I saw him, after shaking hands with me, himself close the door and give a glance to make sure that we were quite alone.

"You must not be astonished at these precautions," he began. "I have some news to tell you which, for reasons which you will understand as soon as you hear what the news is, must be kept secret as long as possible and you know that the walls of a ministerial office have very sharp ears. This is the news: I have just heard from the Russian ambassador and from Delcassé that the negotiations which were on foot between the two governments in view of a second visit of the Tsar and Tsaritsa are at last completed. Their Majesties will pay an official visit of three days to France. They may come to Paris; in any case, they will stay at the Château de Compiègne, where the sovereigns will take up their quarters, together with the President of the Republic and all of us. They will arrive from Russia by sea; they will land at Dunkerque on the 18th of September; and from there they will go straight by rail to Compiègne. The festivities will end with a visit to Rheims and a review of our eastern frontier troops at Bethany Camp."

The minister paused and then continued:

"And now I must ask you to listen to me very carefully. I want *no accident nor incident* of any kind to occur during this visit. The Tsar has been made to believe that his safety and the Tsaritsa's run the greatest risks through their coming to France. It is important that we should give the lie in a striking fashion—as we did in 1896—to this bad reputation which our enemies outside are trying to give us. They are simply working against the alliance; and we have the greatest political interest in defeating their machinations. We must, therefore, take all necessary measures accordingly; and I am entrusting this task to Cavard, the chief of the detective service, Hennion, his colleague, and yourself. You are to divide the work among you. Cavard will control the whole thing and settle the details; Hennion, with his remarkable activity, will see that they are carried out and devote himself to the protection of the Tsar;

and I have reserved for you the most enviable part of the task: I entrust the Empress to your special care."

The Emperor Nicholas II and the Empress Alexandra were very nearly the only members of the Russian Imperial family whom I did not yet know. At the time when they made their first journey to Paris, to celebrate the conclusion of the Franco-Russian alliance, I was in Sweden as the guest of King Oscar, His Majesty having most graciously invited me to spend a period of sick-leave with him; and it was on the deck of his yacht, at the end of a dinner which he gave me in the Bay of Stockholm, that the news of the triumphal reception of the Russian sovereigns had come to gladden my patriotism and his faithful affection for the country which, through his Bernadotte blood, was also his.

On the other hand, I had repeatedly had the honour of attending the grand-dukes; and I was attached to the person of the Tsarevitch George at the time of his two stays on the Côte d'Azur, in the villa which he occupied at the Cap d'Ail, facing the sea, among the orange-trees and thymes. I had beheld the sad and silent tragedy enacted in the mind of that pale and suffering young prince, heir to a mighty empire, whom death had already marked for its own and who knew it! He knew it, but had submitted to fate's decree without a murmur. Resigning himself to the inevitable, he strove to enjoy the few last pleasures that life still held for him: the sunlight, the flowers and the sea; he sought to beguile the anxiety of those about him and of his doctors by assuming a mask of playful good-humour and an appearance of youthful hope and zest. Lastly, at the same Villa des Terrasses, I had known the Dowager-Empress Marie Feodorovna, whom her great green-and-gold train had brought to Russia with her children, the Grand-duchess Xenia and the Grand-duke Michael, at the first news of a slight relapse on the part of the illustrious patient.

For two long months, I took part in the inner life of that little court; and more than once I detected the anguish of the mother stealthily trying to read the secret of her son's hectic eyes, peering at his pale face, watching for his hoarse, hard cough, as he walked beside her, or dined opposite her, or played at cards with his sister, or stroked with his long and too-white hands the head of his lively and slender greyhound, Moustique.

These memories were already four years old. How much had happened since then! The Tsarevitch George had gone to the Caucasus to die; the Franco-Russian alliance, the realisation of which was contemplated in the interviews that took place at the Cap d'Ail between the Dowager Empress and Baron de Mohrenheim, the Russian ambassador in Paris; this alliance might almost already be described as an old marriage, in which the heart has its reasons, of which the reason itself has become aware.

This new visit of the allied sovereigns, therefore, represented an important trump in the game of our policy as against the rest of Europe: it supplied the ready answer which we felt called upon to make from time to time to those who were anxiously waiting for the least event capable of disturbing the intimacy of the Franco-Russian alliance, with a view to exploiting any such event in favour of a rupture.

The reader will easily, therefore, imagine the importance which M. Waldeck-Rousseau attached to his watchword: "No accident nor incident of any kind!"

The measures of protection with which a sovereign is surrounded when he happens to be Emperor of Russia are of a more complicated and delicate character than in the case of any other monarch. Guarded in a formidable manner by his own police, whose brutal zeal, tending as it does to offend and exasperate, is more of a danger than a protection, the Tsar is, unknown to himself, enveloped by the majority of those who hover round him in a network of silent intrigues which keep up a latent spirit of distrust and dismay.

It does not come within my present scope nor do I here intend to frame an indictment against the Russian police. For that matter, tragic incidents and regrettable scandals enough have revealed the sinister and complex underhand methods of that occult force in such a way as to leave no doubt concerning its nature in men's minds. I will content myself with confessing that, although the numberless anonymous letters which we used to receive at the Ministry of the Interior before the Tsar's arrival mostly failed to agitate us, the appearance, on the other hand, of certain tenebrous persons, who came to concert with us as to "the measures to be taken," nearly always resulted in awakening secret terrors within us. I became acquainted in this way, with some of the celebrated "figures" of the Russian secret police: the famous Harting was one of their number; and it is also possible that I may have consorted, without knowing it, with the mysterious Azeff. My clearest recollection of my relations with these gentry—always excepting M. Raskowsky, the chief of the Russian police in Paris—is that we thought it wise to keep them under observation and to hide from them as far as possible the measures which we proposed to adopt for the safety of their sovereigns!

As I have shown above, the responsibility of organising these measures on the occasion of the Tsar's journey in 1901 was entrusted to M. Cavard, the head of the French political police; but the honour of ensuring their proper performance was due above all to M. Hennion, his chief lieutenant, who has now succeeded him. In point of fact, M. Cavard's long and brilliant administrative career had not prepared him for such rough and tiring tasks. An excellent official, this honest man, whose high integrity it is a pleasure to me to recognise, had a better grasp of the sedentary work of the offices. Hennion, on the contrary, "knew his business" and possessed its special qualities. Endowed with a remarkable spirit of initiative and an invariable coolness, eager, indefatigable and shrewd, fond of fighting, with a quick scent for danger, he was always seen in the breach and he knew how to be everywhere at one time. This was an indispensable quality when the zone to be protected extended, as it did in this case, over a length of several hundred miles and embraced almost half France.

In what did these measures consist? First of all, in doubling the watch kept on foreigners living in France and notably on the Russian anarchists. The copious information which we possessed about their antecedents and their movements made our task an easy one. Paris, like every other large city in Europe, contains a pretty active focus of nihilism. This consists mainly of students and of young women, who are generally more formidable than the men. Still, these revolutionary spirits always prefer theory to action and were, consequently, less to be feared than those who, on the pretext of seeing the festivities, might come from abroad charged with a criminal mission.

We had, therefore, established observation-posts in all the frontier stations, posts composed of officers who lost no time in fastening on the steps of any suspicious traveller. But, however minute our investigations might be, it was still possible for the threads of a plot to escape us; and we had to prepare ourselves against possible surprises at places where it was known that the sovereigns were likely to be. A special watch had to be kept along the railways over which the imperial train would travel and in the streets through which the procession would pass. For this purpose, we divided, as usual, the line from Dunkerque to Compiègne and from Compiègne to the frontier into sections and sub-sections, each placed under the command of the district commissary of police, who had under his orders the local police-force and gendarmery, reinforced by the troops stationed in the department. Posted at intervals on either side of the line, at the entrance and issue of the tunnels, on and under the bridges, sentries, with loaded rifles, prevented anyone from approaching and had orders to raise an alarm if they saw that the least suspicious object had, unknown to them, been laid on or near the rails.

We also identified the tenants of all the houses situated either along the railway-line or in the streets through which our guests were to drive. As a matter of fact, what we most feared was the traditional outrage perpetrated or attempted from a window. On the other hand, we refused (contrary to what has been stated) to adopt the system employed by the Spanish, German and Italian police on the occasion of any visit from a sovereign, the system which consists in arresting all the "suspects" during the period of the royal guest's stay. This proceeding not only appeared to us needlessly vexatious, for it constitutes a flagrant attempt upon the liberty of the individual, but we thought that, with our democracy, there was a danger of its alienating the sympathy of our population from our august visitors. We had, therefore, to be content to forestall any possible catastrophes by other and less arbitrary means.

2.

Our vigilance was naturally concentrated with the greatest attention upon Compiègne. We sent swarms of police to beat the forest and search every copse and thicket; and the château itself was inspected from garret to basement by our most trusted detectives. These precautions, however, seemed insufficient to our colleagues of the Russian police. A fortnight before the arrival of the sovereigns, one of them, taking us aside, said:

"The cellars must be watched."

"But it seems to us," we replied, "that we cannot very well do more than we are doing: they are visited every evening; and there are men posted at all the doors."

"Very good; but how do you know that your men will not be bribed and that the 'terrorists' will not succeed, unknown to you, in placing an explosive machine in some dark corner?"

"But what do you suggest, then?"

"Put men upon whom you can rely, here and now, in each cellar, with instructions to remain there night and day until Their Majesties' departure. And, above all, see that they hold no communication with the outside. They must prepare their own meals."

The solution may have been ingenious, but we declined to entertain it; we considered, in point of fact, that it was unnecessary two weeks before the coming of the Emperor and Empress, to condemn a number of decent men to underground imprisonment, a form of torture which had not been inflicted on even the worst criminals for more than a century past.

On the other hand, we mixed some detectives with the numerous staff of workmen who were engaged in restoring the old château to its ancient splendour. The erstwhile imperial residence, which had stood empty since the war, now rose again from its graceful and charming past as though by the stroke of a fairy's wand. The authorities hastily collected the most sumptuous remains of the former furniture now scattered over our museums. Gradually, the deserted halls and abandoned bed-rooms were again filled, in the same places, with the same objects that had adorned them in days gone by. The apartments set aside for the Tsar and Tsaritsa were those once occupied by the Emperors Napoleon I and Napoleon III and the Empresses Marie-Louise and Eugénie. As we passed through them, our eyes were greeted by the wonderful Beauvais tapestries of which the King of Prussia, one day, said that "no king's fortune was large enough to buy them;" we hesitated before treading on the exquisite Savonnerie carpets, with which Louis XIV had covered the floors of Versailles; in the Tsarina's boudoir, we admired Marie-Louise's cheval-glass; in her bed-room we found the proud archduchess's four-poster; in Nicholas II's bed-room, we discovered a relic: the bed of Napoleon I, the beautifully-carved mahogany bedstead in which the man whom a great historian called "that terrible antiquarian" and whom no battle had wearied, dreamt of the empire of Charlemagne. Was it not a striking irony of fate that thus awarded the conqueror's pillow to the first promoter of peaceful arbitration?

While upholsterers, gardeners, carpenters, locksmiths and painters were carrying out the amazing metamorphosis, the ministry was drawing up the programme of the rejoicings and calling in the aid of the greatest poets, the most illustrious artists, the prettiest and most talented ballet-dancers. Rehearsals were held in the theatre where, years ago, the Prince Imperial had made his first appearance; the carriages were tested in the avenues of the park; a swarm of butlers and footmen were taught court etiquette in the servants' hall; and certain ministers' wives, trusting to the discreet solitude of their boudoirs, took lessons in solemn curtseying. It was so many days and weeks of feverish expectation, during which everything had to be improvised for the occasion; for this was the first time since its advent that the Republic was entertaining in the country.

And then the great day came. One morning, on the platform of the Gare du Nord, a gentleman dressed in black, with beard neatly-trimmed, followed by ministers, generals and more persons in black, including myself, stepped into a special train. He had been preceded by a valet carrying three bags. The first—is it not a detective's duty to know everything?—was a dressing-case containing crystal, silver-topped fittings; the second, which was long and flat, held six white shirts, twelve collars, three night-shirts, a pair of slippers and two broad grand-cross ribbons, one red, the other blue; and in the third were packed a brand-new dress-suit, six pairs of white gloves and three pairs of patent-leather boots. M. Loubet, calm and smiling, was starting for Dunkerque to meet his guests.

3.

My first impression of the young sovereigns was very different from that which I expected. To judge by the fantastic measures taken in anticipation of their arrival and by the atmosphere of suspicion and mystery which people had been pleased to create around them, we were tempted to picture them as grave, solemn, haughty, mystical and distrustful; and our thoughts turned, in spite of ourselves to the court of Ivan the Terrible rather than to that of Peter the Great.

Then, suddenly, the impression was changed. When we saw them close at hand, we beheld a very united couple, very simple and kindly, anxious to please everybody and to fall in with everybody's wishes, obviously hating official pomp and ceremony and regretting to be continually separated by impenetrable barriers from the rest of the world. We perceived that they liked to be unreserved, that they were capable of "soulful outbursts" and of endless delicacy of thought, especially for their humbler fellow-citizens. We detected in the laughter in *his* eyes a frank and youthful gaiety that disliked restraint; and we suspected in the melancholy of *hers* the secret tragedy of an ever-anxious affection, of a destiny weighed down by the burden of a crown in which there were all too many thorns and too few roses. And I confess, at the risk of being anathematised by our fierce democrats, that autocracy, as personified by this young couple, who would clearly have been happier between a samovar and a cradle than between a double row of bayonets, that autocracy, under this unexpected aspect, possessed nothing very terrifying and even presented a certain charm.

I think, besides, that an erroneous opinion has been generally formed of the Tsar's character. He has been said and is still said to be a weak man. Now I should be inclined, on this point, to think with M. Loubet that Nicholas II's "weakness" is more apparent than real and that in him, as formerly in our Napoleon III, there is "a gentle obstinate" who has very strong ideas of his own, a being conscious of his power and proud of the glory of his name.

Nicholas II, at the time of his second visit to France, had met M. Loubet before. When the Emperor first came to France, in 1896, the future President of the Republic was president of the Senate and, in this capacity, had not only been presented to the sovereign, but received a visit from him. In this connexion, the late M. Félix Faure used to tell an amusing story, which he said that he had from the Tsar in person.

THE EMPRESS OF RUSSIA AND THE GRAND DUCHESS MARIE

It was after a luncheon at the Élysée. Nicholas II had told President Faure that he would like to call on the president of the Senate and expressed a wish to go to the Palais du Luxembourg, if possible, *incognito*. A landau was at once provided, without an escort; and the Emperor stepped in, accompanied by General de Boisdeffre. At that hour, the peaceful Luxembourg quarter was almost deserted. The people in the streets, expecting the Tsar to drive back from the Russian Embassy, had drifted in that direction to cheer him.

Wishing first to find out if M. Loubet was there, General de Boisdeffre had ordered the coachman to stop a few yards from the palace, opposite the gate of the Luxembourg gardens. He then alighted to go and enquire and to tell the president of the Senate that an august visitor was waiting at his door.

The Tsar, left alone in the carriage and delighted at feeling free and at his ease, looked out of the window with all the zest of a schoolboy playing truant. He saw before him one of those picturesque street-Arabs, who seem to sprout between the paving-stones of Paris. This particular specimen, seated against the railings, was whistling the refrain of the Russian national hymn, with his nose in the air. Suddenly, their eyes met. The wondering street-boy sprang to his feet; he had never seen the Emperor, but he had seen his photographs; and the likeness was striking.

"Suppose it is Nicholas?" he said to himself, greatly puzzled.

And, as he was an inquisitive lad, he resolved to make sure without delay. He took an heroic decision, walked up to within a yard of the carriage and there, bobbing down his head, shouted in a hoarse voice to the unknown foreigner:

"How's the Empress?"

Picture his stupefaction—for, in point of fact, he only thought that he was having a good joke—when he heard the stranger reply, with a smile:

"Thank you, the Empress is very well and is delighted with her journey."

The boy, then and there, lost his tongue. He stared at the speaker in dismay; and then, after raising his cap, stalked away slowly, very slowly, to mark his dignity.

Nicholas II retained a delightful recollection of this private interview with a true Parisian and long amused himself by scandalising the formal set around him with the story of this adventure.

4.

If, on his second stay, he did not have the occasion of coming into contact with the people, he none the less enjoyed the satisfaction of being admirably received.

The episodes of the first day of this memorable visit, from the moment when, on the deck of the *Standart*, lying off Dunkerque, the sovereigns, as is customary whenever they leave their yacht, received the salute of the sailors and the blessing of the old priest in his violet cassock: these episodes have been too faithfully chronicled in the press for me to linger over them here. It was a magnificent landing, amid the thunder of the guns and the hurrahs of the enthusiastic populace. Then came the journey from Dunkerque to Compiègne, a real triumphal progress, in which the cheers along the line seemed to travel almost as fast as the train, for they were linked from town to town, from village to village, from farm to farm. At last came the arrival, at nightfall, in the little illuminated town, followed by the torch-light procession, in which the fantastic figure of the red cossack stood out, as he clung to the back of the Empress's carriage; the entrance into the courtyard of the château all ablaze with light; the slow ascent of the staircases lined with cuirassiers, standing immovable, with drawn swords, and powdered footmen, in blue liveries *à la française*,[2] and, lastly, the presentations, enlivened, at a certain moment by the artless question which a minister's wife, in a great state of excitement and anxious to please addressed to the Empress:

"How are your little ones?"

5.

Although from the time of leaving Dunkerque, I had taken up my duties, which, as the reader knows, consisted more particularly in ensuring the personal safety of the Empress, I had as yet only caught a glimpse of that gracious lady. A few hours after our arrival at the château, chance made me come across her and she deigned to speak to me. I doubt whether she observed my state of flurry; and yet, that evening, without knowing it, she was the cause of a strange hallucination of my mind.

I had left the procession at the entrance to the drawing-rooms, in order to go and ascertain if our orders had been faithfully carried out in and around the imperial apartments. Gradually, as I penetrated into the maze of long silent corridors, filled with my own officers, impassive in their footmen's liveries, a crowd of confused memories rose in my brain. I remembered a certain evening, similar to the present, when the palace was all lit up for a celebration. I, at that time, still a young student, had come to see my kinsman, Dr. Conneau, physician to the Emperor Napoleon III. We went along the same corridors together, when, suddenly holding me back by the sleeve and pointing to a proud and radiant, fair-haired figure which at that moment passed through the vivid brightness of a distant gallery, he said:

"The Empress!"

Now, at the same spot, forty years after, another voice, that of one of my inspectors, came and whispered in my ear:

"The Empress!"

I started; in front of me, at the end of the gallery, a figure, also radiant and also fair, had suddenly come into view. Was it a dream, a fairy-tale? No, there was another empress, that was all; in the same frame in which, as a boy, I had first set eyes upon the Empress Eugénie, I now saw the Empress Alexandra coming towards me. I was so much taken aback that, at first, I stood rooted to the spot, seeking to recover my presence of mind. She continued her progress, proceeding to her apartments followed by her ladies-in-waiting. When she was at a few yards from the place where I stood motionless, her eyes fell upon me; then she came up to me and, holding out her white and slender hand:

"I am glad to see you, M. Paoli," she said, "for I know how highly my dear grandmother, Queen Victoria, used to think of you."

What she did not know was how often Queen Victoria had spoken of her to me. That great sovereign, in fact, cherished a special affection for the child of her idolised daughter, the Grand-duchess Alice of Hesse. The child reminded her of the happy time when the princess wrote to her from Darmstadt, on the day after the birth of the future Empress of Russia:

"She is the personification of her nickname, 'Sunny,' much like Ella, but a smaller head, and livelier, with Ernie's dimple and expression."

Then, a few days later:

"We think of calling her Alix (Alice they pronounce too dreadfully in Germany) Helena Louisa Beatrice; and, if Beatrice may, we would like her to have her for godmother."

And these letters, so pretty, so touching, continued through the years that followed. The baby had grown into a little girl, the little girl into a young girl; and her mother kept Queen Victoria informed of the least details concerning the child. She was anxious, fond and proud by turns; and she asked for advice over and over again:

"I strive to bring her up totally free from pride of her position, which is nothing save what her personal merit can make it. I feel so entirely as you do on the difference of rank and how all important it is for Princes and Princesses to know that they are nothing better or above others save through their own merit and that they have only the double duty of living for others and of being an example, good and modest."

Next come more charming details. Princess Alice, returning to her children at Darmstadt after a visit to England, writes to the Queen:

"They eat me up! They had made wreaths over the doors and had no end of things to tell me....

"We arrived at three and there was not a moment's rest till they were all in bed and I had heard the different prayers of the six, with all the different confidences they had to make."

Elsewhere, interesting particulars about the education of Princess Alix, an exclusively English education, very simple and very healthy, the programme of which included every form of physical exercise, such as bicycling, skating, tennis and riding, and allowed her, by way of pocket-money, 50 pfennigs a week between the ages of 4 and 8; 1 mark from 8 to 12; and 2 marks from 12 to 16 years.

In the twenty-nine years that had passed since the first of these letters was written, what a number of events had occurred!

Princess Alice, that admirable mother, had died from giving a kiss to her son Ernie, when he was suffering from diphtheria; the royal grandmother, in her turn, had died quite recently. Of the seven children whose gaiety brightened the domestic charm of the little court at Darmstadt, two had perished in a tragic fashion: Prince Fritz, first, killed by an accidental fall from a window, while playing with his brother; and Princess May, carried off in twenty-four hours, she, too, by diphtheria caught at the bedside of her sister "Aliky," the present Empress of Russia. As for the other "dear little ones," as Queen Victoria called them, they had all been dispersed by fate. "Ella" had become the Grand-duchess Serge of Russia; "Enric" had succeeded his father on the throne of Hesse; two of his sisters had married, one Prince Henry of Prussia, the other Prince Louis of Battenberg; and the last had become the wearer of the heaviest of all crowns. And now chance placed her here, before me.

I looked at her with, in my mind, the memory of all the letters which an august and kindly condescension had permitted me to read and of the gentle emotion with which the good and great Queen used to speak of the Princess Alice and of her daughter, the present Empress of Russia. Her features had not yet acquired, under the imperial diadem, that settled air of melancholy which the obsession of a perpetual danger was to give her later; in the brilliancy of her full-blown youth, which set a gladsome pride upon the tall, straight forehead; in the golden sheen of her queenly hair; in her grave and limpid blue eyes, through which shot gleams of sprightliness; in her smile, still marked by the dimples of her girlish days, I recognised her to whom the fond imagination of a justly-proud mother had awarded, in her cradle, the pretty nickname of "Sunny."

She stopped before me for a few moments. Before moving away, she said:

"I believe you are commissioned to 'look after' me?"

"That is so," I replied.

"I hope," she added, laughing, "that I shall not give you too much worry."

I dared not confess to her that it was not only worry, but perpetual anguish that her presence and the Tsar's were causing me.

6.

We had to be continually on the watch, to have safe men at every door, in every passage, on every floor; we had to superintend the least details. I remember, for instance, standing by for nearly two hours while the Empress's dresses were being unpacked, so great was our fear lest a disguised bomb might be slipped into one of the sovereign's numerous trunks, while the women were arranging the gowns in the special presses and cupboards intended for them. Lastly, day and night, we had to go on constant rounds, both inside and outside the château.

On the occasion of one of these minute investigations, I met with a rather interesting adventure. Not far from the apartments reserved for the Empress Alexandra's ladies was an unoccupied room, the door of which was locked. It appeared that, during the Empire, this room had been used by Madame Bruant, the Prince Imperial's governess, wife of Admiral Bruant. At a time when every apartment in the château was thrown open for the visit of our imperial guests, why did this one alone remain closed? I was unable to say. In any case, my duty obliged me to leave no corner unexplored; and, on the first evening, I sent for a bunch of keys. After a few ineffectual attempts, the lock yielded, the door opened ... and imagine my bewilderment! In a charming disorder, tin soldiers, dancing dolls, rocking horses and beautiful picture-books lay higgledy-piggledy in the middle of the room, around a great, big, ugly plush bear!

I enquired and found that they were the Prince Imperial's toys: they had been left there and forgotten for thirty years. And an interesting coincidence was that the big bear was the last present made by the Tsar Alexander II to the little prince.

I softly closed the door which I had opened upon the past; I resolved to respect those playthings; there are memories which it is better not to awaken.

The next morning chance allowed me to assist at a sight which many a photographer would have been glad to "snap." The Tsar and Tsaritsa, who are both very early risers, had gone down to the garden, accompanied by their great greyhound, which answered to the name of Lofki. The Tsar was expected to go shooting that morning, in anticipation of which intention the keepers had spent the night in filling the park with pheasants, deer and hares. Their labours were wasted; Nicholas II preferred to stroll round the lawns with the Empress. She was bare-headed and had simply put up a parasol against the sun, which was of dazzling brightness; she carried a camera slung over her shoulder. The young couple, whom I followed hidden behind a shrubbery, turned their steps towards the covered walk of hornbeams which Napoleon I had had made for Marie-Louise, hoping, no doubt, to find in the shade of this beautiful leafy vault, which autumn was already decking with its copper hues, a discreet solitude suited to the billing and cooing of the pair of lovers that they were. But the departments of public ceremony and public safety were on the lookout; already, inside the bosky tunnel, fifty soldiers commanded by a lieutenant, were presenting arms!

The sovereigns had to make the best of a bad job. The Emperor reviewed the men with a serious face and the Empress photographed them and promised to send the lieutenant a print as soon as the plate was developed. Thereupon the Tsar and Tsaritsa walked away in a different direction. A charming little wood appeared before their eyes. Lofki was running ahead of them. Suddenly, a furious barking was heard; and four gendarmes emerged from behind a clump of fir-trees and, presenting arms, gave the military salute!

There was nothing to be done and the sovereigns gaily accepted the situation. With a merry burst of laughter, they turned on their heels and resolved to go back to the château. By way of consolation, the Tsaritsa amused herself by photographing her husband, who, in his turn, took a snapshot of his wife.

They showed no bitterness on account of the disappointment which their walk must have caused them. In fact, to anybody who asked him, on his return, if he had enjoyed his stroll, Nicholas II contented himself with saying:

"Oh, yes, the grounds are beautiful; and I now know what you mean by 'a well-cared-for property'!"

7.

While life was being arranged in the great palace and everyone settling down as if he were to stay there for a month instead of three days; while the head of the kitchens, acting under the inspiration of the head of the ceremonial department, was cudgelling his brains to bring his menus into harmony with politics by introducing subtle alliances of French and Russian dishes; while the musicians were tuning their violins for the "gala" concert of the evening and Mme. Bartet, that divine actress, preparing to utter, in her entrancing voice, M. Edmund Rostand's famous lines beginning, "Oh! Oh! *Voici une impératrice!*"[3] while the Tsaritsa, at first a little lost amid these new surroundings, found a friend in the Marquise de Montebello, our agreeable ambassadress in St. Petersburg, of whom people used to say that she justified Turgenev's epigram when he declared that, wherever you see a Frenchwoman, you see all France; while the most complete serenity seemed to reign among the inhabitants of the château, a solemn question was stirring all men's minds. Would the Tsar go to Paris? As it was, the people of Paris were disappointed because the reception had not been held in the capital, as in 1896; would he give it the compensation of a few hours' visit? A special train was awaiting, with steam up, in the station at Compiègne; long confabulations took place between the Emperor and M. Waldeck-Rousseau; a luncheon was prepared at the Élysée with a view to the entertainment of an illustrious guest; secret orders were given to the police. In short, nobody doubted that Nicholas II intended to carry out a plan which everybody ascribed to him.

Nothing came of it. The Tsar did not go to Paris.

This sudden change of purpose was interpreted in different ways. Some people pretended that the prime minister was at the bottom of it, M. Waldeck-Rousseau having declared that he could not answer for the Emperor's safety in view of the inadequate nature of the preparations. In reality, we never learnt the true reasons; and I have often asked myself whether this regrettable decision should not be attributed to the influence of "Philippe."

Who was "Philippe"? A strange, disconcerting being, who had something of the quack about him and something of the prophet and who followed the Tsar like a shadow.

His story was an astounding one from start to finish. He was a native of Lyons—a Frenchman, therefore—who pretended, with the assistance of mystical practices and of inner voices which he summoned forth and consulted, to be able to cure maladies, to forestall dangers, to foresee future events. He gave consultations and wrote prescriptions, for he did not reject the aid of science. And, as he came within the law which forbids the illegal practice of medicine, he hit upon the obvious expedient of marrying his daughter to a doctor, who acted as his man of straw. His waiting-room was never empty from the day when the Grand-duke Nicholas Michaelovitch, chancing to pass through Lyons and to hear of this mysterious personage, thought that he would consult him about his rheumatism. What happened? This much is certain, that the grand-duke, on returning to Russia, declared that Philippe had cured him as though by magic and that he possessed the power not only of driving out pain, but of securing the fulfilment of every wish. The Emperor, at that time, was longing for an heir. Greatly impressed by his cousin's stories and by his profound conviction, he resolved to summon the miracle-monger to St. Petersburg. This laid the foundation of Philippe's fortunes. Admirably served by his lucky star, highly intelligent, gifted with the manners of an apostle and an appearance of absolute disinterestedness, he gradually succeeded in acquiring a considerable hold not only on the imperial family, but on the whole court. People began to believe very seriously in his supernatural powers. Made much of and respected, he had free access to the sovereigns and ended by supplanting both doctors and advisers. He also treated cases at a distance, by auto-suggestion. Whenever he obtained leave to go home on a visit, he kept up with his illustrious clients an exchange of telegrams that would tend to make us smile, if they did not stupefy us at the thought of so much credulity. Thus, a given person of quality would wire:

"Suffering violent pains head entreat give relief."

Whereupon Philippe would at once reply:

"Have concentrated thought on pain; expect cure between this and five o'clock to-morrow."

This is not an invention: I have seen the telegrams.

For people to have so blind a faith in his mediation, he must obviously have effected a certain number of cures. As a matter of fact, I believe that the power of the will is such that, in certain affections which depended partly upon the nervous system, he succeeded in suggesting to a patient that he was not and could not be ill.

However, what was bound to happen, happened. His star declined from the day when people became persuaded that he was not infallible. The Tsar's set precipitated his disgrace when the Tsaritsa brought another daughter into the world, instead of the promised son. One fine day, Philippe went back to Lyons for good; he died there a few years ago. And, in the following year, the mighty empire had an heir!

At the time of the visit of the sovereigns to Compiègne, he was still at the height of his favour. He accompanied our imperial hosts; and his presence at the château surprised us as much as anything. In fact, like the Doge of Venice who came to Versailles under Louis XIV, he himself might have said:

"What astonishes me most is to see myself here!"

But Philippe was astonished at nothing. Anxious to retain his personality in the midst of that gold-laced crowd, he walked about the apartments in a grey suit and brown shoes; on the first day, he was within an ace of being arrested; we took him for an anarchist!

Our extreme distrust, to which the unfortunate Philippe nearly fell a victim, was only too well justified. I believe that I am not guilty of an indiscretion—for the memorable events of 1901 are now a matter of history—when I say to-day that there was an attempt, an attempt of which our guests never heard, because a miraculous accident enabled us to defeat its execution in the nick of time.

It was in the cathedral of Rheims that the criminal effort was to be accomplished during the visit of the sovereigns, who had expressed a desire to see the inside of that exquisite fabric. On learning of Their Majesties' intention, our colleagues of the Russian police displayed the greatest nervousness:

"Nothing could be easier," they told us, a few days before the visit, "than for a Terrorist to deposit a bomb in some dark place, under a chair, behind a confessional, or at the foot of a statue. The interior of the cathedral must be watched from this moment, together with the people who enter it."

Although we had already thought of this, they decided, on their part, to entrust this task to an "informer"—in other words, a spy—of Belgian nationality, who had joined the Russian detective-service. Hennion, who was always prudent, hastened, in his turn, to set a watch on the "informer." Twenty-four hours later, one of his men came to see him in a great state of fright:

"M. Hennion," he said, "I have obtained proof that the 'informer' is connected with a gang of Terrorists. They are preparing an attack in the cathedral!"

Hennion did not hesitate for a moment. He hastened to Rheims, instituted a police-search in a room which the "informer" had secretly hired under a false name and seized a correspondence which left no doubt whatever as to the existence of the plot. The "informer" himself was to do the dirty work!

He was at once arrested and pressed with questions:

"I swear that I know nothing about it," he exclaimed, "and that's the plain truth!"

"Very well," said Hennion, who held absolute proof. "Take this man to prison," he ordered, "since he's telling the truth, and drag him back to me when he decides to tell a lie."

The next day, the man confessed.

This was the only tragic episode that occurred during the imperial visit. Nevertheless, in spite of the satisfaction which we had felt at receiving the Tsar and Tsaritsa, we heaved a sigh of relief when, on the following day, we saw the train that was to take them back to Russia steam out of the station.

They were still alive, God be praised! But that was almost more than could be said of us!

V

THE KING AND QUEEN OF ITALY

1.

I have always harboured a vagrant spirit under my official frock-coat. I find my pleasure and my rest in travelling. I, therefore, took advantage of a few weeks' leave of absence, allowed me after the departure of the Russian sovereigns, to pay a visit to Italy.

A few days after my arrival at Milan, I was strolling, one afternoon, on the well-known Galleria Vittorio Emmanuele, that favourite Milanese and cosmopolitan resort, whose incessant and picturesque animation presages the gaiety, if not the charm of Italy, when the window of a glove-shop caught my eye and reminded me that I had left my gloves in the railway-carriage. I thought I might as well buy myself a new pair; and I entered the shop. A customer had gone in before me. It was a lady, young, tall and slender, quietly but elegantly dressed in a plain, dark travelling-frock. Through the long blue motor-veil that close-shrouded her face and even her hat, a pair of eyes gleamed, black and, as I thought, large and beautiful; her hair was dark and, as far as I could see, she had masses of it; the face seemed refined and pretty. Leaning on the counter, she tried on the gloves which a young shop-assistant handed to her. None of them fitted her.

"They are too large," she said, shyly.

"That is because the signora has so small a hand," replied the young assistant, gallantly.

She smiled and did not answer; the elderly lady who was with her gave the youth an indignant and scandalised glance. After patiently allowing the measure to be taken of her hand, open and closed—it was indeed a very small one—she ended by finding two pairs of gloves to suit her, paid for them and went out.

Just then, the owner of the shop returned. He looked at the lady, gave a bewildered start, bowed very low and, as soon as she was gone, shouted to his assistant:

"Have you the least idea whom you have been serving?"

"A very pretty woman, I know that!"

"Idiot! It was the Queen!"

The Queen! It was my turn to feel bewildered. The Queen, alone, unprotected, in that arcade full of people! I was on the point of following her, from professional habit, forgetting that I was at Milan not as an official, but as a private tourist. A still more important reason stopped my display of zeal: it was too late; the charming vision was lost in the crowd.

2.

The next evening, I was dining at a friend's house, where the guests belonged, for the most part, to the official and political world. When I related my adventure and expressed my astonishment at having met the sovereign making her own purchases in town, accompanied by a stern lady-in-waiting:

"Did that surprise you?" I was asked. "It does not surprise us at all. One of our haughty princesses of the House of Savoy said, sarcastically, that we had gone back to the times when kings used to mate with shepherdesses. This was merely a disrespectful sally. The truth is that both our King and Queen have very simple tastes and that they like to live as ordinary people, in so far as their obligations permit them. Let me give you an instance in point; whenever they come to Milan—and they never stay for more than two or three days—they go to the royal palace, of course, but, instead of living in the state apartments and bringing a large number of servants, they prefer to occupy just a few rooms, have their meals sent in from the Ristorante Cova and order the dishes to be all brought up at the same time and placed on a sideboard. Then they dismiss the servants, shut the doors and wait upon themselves."

In our sunny countries—I can speak for them, as a Corsican—we love pomp and ceremony. I seemed to observe in the friends who gave me this striking illustration of the royal simplicity a touch of bitterness, perhaps of regret. Remarks that came to my ears later led me to the conclusion that the aristocracy, if not the people, disapproved of their sovereign's democratic tendencies, which contrasted with the ways of the old court, of which Queen Margherita had been the soul and still remained the living and charming embodiment.

No doubt. Queen Helena's "manner" was entirely different from that of Margherita of Savoy, whose highly-developed and refined culture, whose apposite wit, whose engaging mode of address, built up of shades that appealed to delicate minds, had attracted to the Quirinal the pick of intellectual, artistic and literary Italy and held it bound in fervent admiration. Educated at the court of her father, Prince Nicholas, Helena of Montenegro had grown up amid the austere scenery of her native land, in constant contact with the rugged simplicity of the Montenegrin highlanders; her wide-open child-eyes had never rested on other than grave and manly faces; her girlhood was decked not with fairy-tales, but with the old, wild legends of the mountains, or else, with epics extolling the heroism of those who, in the days of old, had driven the foreign invader from the valleys of Antivari or the lofty plateaux of Cetinje. At the age of twelve, she was sent to St. Petersburg to finish her studies. There, in the promiscuous intercourse of a convent confined to young ladies of gentle birth, she had known the charm of friendships that removed all differences of social rank between her fellow schoolgirls and herself, while her mind opened to the somewhat melancholy beauties of Slav literature. On returning to her country, she enjoyed, in the fulness of an independence wholly undisturbed by the demand of etiquette, the healthy delights of an open-air life, which she divided between watercolour drawing, in which she excelled, and sport in which she showed herself fearless.

When, therefore, she saw Italy for the first time in 1895 and saw it through the gates of Venice, where her father had taken her on the occasion of an exhibition; when, one evening, in the midst of the fanciful and to her novel scene of the lagoon arrayed in its holiday attire, she saw the homage of a glowing admiration in the eyes of the then Prince of Naples, it will readily be conceived that she was flurried and a little dazzled. When, lastly, in the following year, she bade farewell to her craggy mountains and to the proud highlanders, the companions of her childhood, and saw the gay and enthusiastic nation of Italy hastening to welcome her, the twenty-years-old bride, with the hopes and promises which she brought with her, it will be understood that she at first experienced a sense of confusion and shyness.

The shyness, I am told, has never completely worn off. On the other hand, in the absence of more brilliant outward qualities, Queen Helena has displayed admirable domestic virtues; she has known how to be a queen in all that this function implies in regard to noble and delicate missions of devotion and goodness to the poor and lowly. And she has done better than that: she has realised her engrossing duties as wife and mother; and they are sweet and dear to her.

Had this been otherwise, the King's character, which is quick to take offence, and his jealous fondness would have suffered cruelly. He too is shy, he too is a man of domestic habits, who has always avoided society and pleasure. Possessing none of the physical qualities that attract the crowd, endowed with an unimaginative, but, on the other hand, a reflective and studious mind, remarkably well-informed, highly-intelligent, passionately enamoured of social problems and the exact sciences, none was readier than he to enjoy the charm of a peaceful home which he had not known during his youth. Touching, in fact, though the attachment between the son and mother was, they nevertheless remained separated by the differences in their character, their temperament and their ideas. Whereas Queen Margherita kept all her enthusiasm for art and literature, the Prince of Naples displayed, if not a repugnance, at least a complete indifference to such matters. When he was only ten years of age, he said to his piano-mistress, Signora Cerasoli, who was appointed by his mother and who vainly struggled to instil the first principles of music into his mind:

"Don't you think that twenty trumpets are more effective than that piano of yours?"

To make amends, he showed from his earliest youth a marked predilection for military science. He had the soul of a soldier and submitted, without a murmur, to the strict discipline imposed upon him by his tutor, Colonel Osio. He is still fond of relating, as one of the pleasantest memories of his life, the impression which he felt on the day when King Humbert first entrusted him with the command of a company of foot at the annual review of the Roman garrison:

"The excitement interfered so greatly with my power of sight," he says, "that the only people I recognised in the cheering crowd were my dentist and my professor of mathematics."

His keen love of the army became manifest when, as heir apparent, he received the command of the army-corps of Naples. Frivolous and light-headed Neapolitan society looked forward to receiving a worldly-minded prince and rejoiced accordingly; but it soon discovered its mistake; the prince, scorning pleasure, devoted himself exclusively to his profession and left his barracks only to go straight back to the Capodimonte Palace, where he spent his spare time in perfecting himself in the study of military tactics.

When, at last, the tragedy of Monza called him suddenly to the throne, the manliness of his attitude, the firmness of his character and the soberness of his mind impressed the uneasy and scattered world of politics. He insisted upon drawing up his first proclamation to the Italian people with his own hand and in it proved himself a man of the times, thoroughly acquainted with the needs and aspirations of modern Italy.

"I know," he said to Signor Crispi, a few days after his accession, "I know all the responsibilities of my station and I would not presume to think that I can remedy the present difficulties with my own unaided strength. But I am convinced that those difficulties all spring from one cause. In Italy, there are few citizens who perform their duty strictly: there is too much indolence, too much laxity. Italy is at a serious turning-point in her history; she is eaten up with politics; she must absolutely direct her energies towards the development of her economic resources. Her industries will save her by improving her financial position and employing all the hands at present lying idle in an inactivity that has lasted far too long. I shall practise what I preach by scrupulously following my trade as king and by encouraging initiative, especially by encouraging the social and economic evolution of the country."

Let me do him this justice: he has kept his promises. A will soon made itself conspicuous under that frail exterior. He applied to the consideration of every subject the ardour of an insatiable curiosity and his wish to know things correctly and thoroughly. He studied the confused conditions of Italian parliamentary life with as much perseverance as the social question. It is possible that, by democratising the monarchy, he has forestalled popular movements which, in a country so passionate in its opinions and so exuberant in its manifestations as Italy, might have caused irreparable disorders and delayed the magnificent progress of the nation.

Pondering over these serious problems, his vigilant and studious mind sought relaxation and, at times, consolation and encouragement for its rough task in the ever-smiling intimacy of the home. It resolved that this home should be impenetrable to others, so impenetrable that it excluded the sovereign and *à fortiori* his official "set": the husband and father alone are admitted. This is the secret of that close union which has made people say of the Italian royal couple that they represent the perfect type of a middle-class household which found its way by accident into a king's palace.

I have tried to give a psychological picture of the two sovereigns arising from the impressions which I picked up in the course of my trip to Italy. Their visit to Paris was destined to confirm its accuracy and to complete its details.

3.

I little thought, on the afternoon when I caught so unexpected a glimpse of Queen Helena in a Milan glove-shop, that, two years later, I was to have the honour of attending both Her Majesty and the King during their journey to France. It was their first visit to Paris in state; and our government attached considerable importance to this event, which accentuated the scope of what Prince von Bülow, at that time chancellor of the German Empire, called, none too good-humouredly, Italy's "little waltz" with France.

THE KING AND QUEEN OF ITALY

The letter of appointment which I received at the beginning of October, 1903, directed me to go at once and await our guests at the Italian frontier and bring them safely to Paris. It was pitch-dark, on a cold, wet night, when the royal train steamed out of the Mont-Cenis tunnel and pulled up at the platform of the frontier-station of Modany where I had been pacing up and down for over an hour. My curiosity was stimulated, I must confess, by the recollection of the episode in the Galleria Vittorio Emmanuele at Milan. Amused by the chance which was about to bring me face to face with "the lady with the gloves," I was longing to know if my first impressions were correct and if the features which I had conjectured, rather than perceived, behind the blue veil were really those which I should soon be able to view in the full light.

The blinds of the eight royal railway-carriages were lowered; not a sign betrayed the presence of living beings in the silent train.

After a long moment, a carriage-door opened and a giant, in a long pale-grey cavalry cloak and a blue forage-cap braided with scarlet piping and adorned with a gold tassel, stepped out softly and, making straight for me, said:

"Hush! They are asleep."

It was two o'clock in the morning. The first official reception had been arranged to take place at Dijon, where we were due to arrive at nine o'clock. I took my seat in the train and we started. Not everybody was asleep. In the last carriage, which was reserved for the servants, a number of maids, wrapped in those beautiful red shawls which you see on the quays at Naples, were chattering away, with the greatest animation, in Italian. The echoes of that musical and expressive language reached the compartment in which I was trying to doze and called up memories of my childhood in my old Corsican heart.

It was broad daylight and we were nearing Dijon when Count Guicciardini, the King's master of the horse, came to fetch me to present me to the sovereigns.

Two black, grave, proud and gentle eyes; a forehead framed in a wealth of dark hair; beautiful and delicate features; a smile that produced two little dimples on either side of the mouth; a tall, slight figure; I at once recognised the lady of Milan in the charming sovereign, stately and shy, who came stepping towards me. It was the same little white hand that she put out again, this time, however, that I might press upon it the homage of my respectful welcome. Should I recall the incident of the gloves? I had it on my lips to do so. I was afraid of appearing ridiculous; of course, she did not remember. I said nothing.

"Delighted, M. Paoli, delighted to know you!" exclaimed the King, fixing me with his piercing eyes and shaking me vigorously by the hand.

"Sir."

"But stay; Paoli is an Italian name!"

"Very nearly, Sir; I am a Corsican."

"A fellow-countryman of Napoleon's, then? I congratulate you!"

Our conversation, that morning, was limited to these few words. From Dijon onwards, the journey assumed an official character; and I lost sight of the King and Queen amid the crowd of glittering uniforms. However, a few minutes before our arrival at Paris, I surprised them both standing against a window-pane, the Queen in an exquisite costume of pale-grey velvet and silk, the King in the uniform of an Italian general, with the broad ribbon of the Legion of Honour across his chest. While watching the landscape, they exchanged remarks that appeared to me to be of an affectionate nature.

Meanwhile, a sedate footman entered and discreetly placed upon the table, behind the sovereigns, an extraordinary object that attracted my eyes. It looked like an enormous bird buried in its feathers; it was at one and the same time resplendent and voluminous. I came closer and then saw that it was a helmet, just a helmet, covered with feathers of fabulous dimensions. I was not the only one, for that matter, to be astonished at the imposing proportions of this head-dress; whenever the King donned it in Paris, it met with a huge success; it towered above the crowds, the livery-servants' cockades, the soldiers' bayonets; it became the target of every kodak.

The Queen's shyness? The occasion soon offered to observe it; in fact, that solemn entry into Paris was enough to make any young woman, queen or no queen, shy. The authorities wished it to be as grand as possible and sent the procession down the Avenue du Bois de Boulogne and the Champs-Élysées. No doubt, the charming sovereign was deeply impressed and a little bewildered; but the warmth of her welcome, the heartiness of the cheering afforded her, as well as her consort, a visible pleasure; and, from that very first day, she was full of pretty thoughts and he of generous movements. At a certain moment, she took a rose from a bouquet of *roses de France* which she was carrying and gave it to a little girl who had thrust herself close up to the carriage. He, on the other hand, walked straight to the colours of the battalion of Zouaves who were presenting arms in the courtyard of the Foreign Office and raised to his lips the folds of the standard on which were inscribed two names dear to Italian hearts and French memories alike: Magenta and Solferino.

The Foreign Office was turned into a "royal palace" for the occasion of this visit. While the government had set its wits to work to decorate in the most sumptuous style the apartments which the King and Queen of Italy were to occupy on the first floor, Madame Delcassé, the wife of the foreign minister, on her side, did her best to relieve the somewhat cold and solemn appearance of the rooms. With this object, she procured photographs of the little Princesses Yolanda and Mafalda and placed them in handsome frames on the Queen's dressing-table. The Queen was greatly touched by the delicate attention. On entering the room, she uttered a spontaneous exclamation that betrayed all a mother's fondness:

"Oh, the children! How delightful!"

The children! How often those words returned to her lips during her stay in Paris! She spoke of them incessantly, she spoke of them to everybody, to Madame Loubet, to Madame Delcassé, to the Italian ambassadress, even to the two French waiting-maids attached to her service:

"Yolanda, the elder, with her black hair and her black eyes is like me," she would explain. "Mafalda, on the other hand, is the image of her father. They both have such good little hearts."

Her maternal anxiety was also manifested in the impatience with which she used to wait for news of the princesses. Every evening, when she returned to the Foreign Office after a day of drives and visits in different parts of Paris, her first words were:

"My wire?"

And, a little nervously, she opened the telegram that wras dispatched to her daily from San Rossore, where "the children" were, and greedily read the bulletin of reassuring news which it contained.

On the morning after her arrival, she rang for a maid as soon as she woke up:

"I have an old friend in Paris," she said, "whom I want to see; it is my old French mistress, Mlle. E——. She lives on the Quai Voltaire; please have her sent for."

An attaché of the office hastened off at once and, in half an hour, returned triumphantly with Mlle. E——, a charming old lady who had once been governess to Princess Helena of Montenegro at Cetinje. She had not seen her for ten years; and the reader can imagine her surprise and her confusion. The mistress and pupil threw themselves into each other's arms. And, when Mlle. E—— persisted in addressing the Queen as "Your Majesty," the latter interrupted her and said:

"Why 'Your Majesty'? Call me Helena, as in the old days."

The authorities, conforming to royal usage, had considered it the proper thing to prepare two distinct suites of rooms, one for the King and one for the Queen, separated by an enormous drawing-room. Great was our surprise when, on the following morning, the rumour ran through the passages of the Foreign Office that the King's bed-room had remained untenanted. Had he found it uncomfortable? Did he not like the room? Everyone began to be anxious and it was felt that the mystery must be cleared up. I therefore went to one of the officers of the royal suite, took him aside and, while talking of "other things," tried to question him as to the King's impressions:

"Is His Majesty pleased with his apartments?"

"Delighted."

"Was there anything wrong with the heating arrangements?"

"No, nothing."

"Perhaps the King does not care for the bed provided for His Majesty's use? I hear it is very soft and comfortable, in addition to being historic."

"Not at all, not at all; I believe His Majesty thought everything perfect."

Alas, I felt that my hints were misunderstood! I must needs speak more directly. Without further circumlocution, therefore, I said:

"The fact is, it appears that the King did not deign to occupy his apartment."

The officer looked at me and smiled:

"But the King never leaves the Queen!" he exclaimed. "With us, married couples seldom have separate rooms, unless when they are on bad terms. And that is not the case here!..."

They never were parted, in fact, except at early breakfast. The King was accustomed to take *café au lait*, the Queen chocolate; the first was served in the small sitting-room, where the King, already dressed in his general's uniform, went through his letters; the second in the boudoir, where the Queen, in a pink surat dressing-gown, trimmed with lace, devoted two hours, after her toilet, every morning, to her correspondence, or to the very feminine pleasure of trying on frocks and hats.

I twice again had the honour of seeing her shopping, as on a former celebrated occasion; but this time I accompanied her in the course of my professional duties. She bought no gloves, but made up for it by purchases of linen, jewels, numerous knick-knacks and toys; and one would have thought that she was buying those china dolls, with their tiny sets of tea-things, for herself, so great was the child-like joy which she showed in their selection.

"This is for Yolanda; this is for Mafalda," she said, as she pointed to the objects that were to be placed on one side.

I saw her for the first time grave and thoughtful at the Palace at Versailles, which she and the King visited in the company of M. and Madame Loubet. I think that she must have retained a delightful recollection of this excursion to the palace of our kings, an excursion which left a lively impression on my mind. It seemed as though Nature herself had conspired to accentuate its charm. The ancestral park was as it were shrouded in the soft rays of the expiring autumn: the trees crowned their sombre tops with a few belated leaves of golden brown; the distances were mauve, like lilac in April; and the breeze that blew from the west scattered the water of the fountains and changed it into feathery tufts of vapour.

The sovereigns, escorted by the distinguished keeper of the palace, M. de Noblac, first visited the state apartments, stopping for some time before the portraits of the princes and princesses of the House of France. And, in those great rooms filled with so many precious memories, Queen Helena listened silently and eagerly to the keeper's explanations. She lingered more particularly in the private apartments of Marie Antoinette, where the most trifling objects excited her curiosity; obviously her imagination as a woman and a queen took pleasure in this feminine and royal past. Sometimes, obeying a discreet and spontaneous impulse, when the overpowering memory of some tragic episode weighed too heavily upon our silent thoughts, she pressed herself timidly against the King, as a little girl might do. And once we heard her whisper:

"Ah, if things could speak!"

4.

And the King? The King, while appreciating, as an expert, the archæological beauties which we had to show him and the imperishable evidences of our history, did not share the Queen's enthusiasm for our artistic treasures. When coming to Paris, he had looked forward to two chief pleasures: to see our soldiers and to visit the Musée Monétaire, or collection of coins at our national mint.

As is well-known, Victor Emanuel is considered—and rightly so—an exceedingly capable numismatist. He is very proud of his title as honorary president of the Italian Numismatical Society and, in 1897, undertook the task of drawing up the catalogue of the authentic old coinages of Italy. He derived the necessary materials for his work from his own collection, which at that time consisted of about forty thousand pieces. Now, of the two hundred and sixty types of Italian coinage known, barely one-half could lay claim to absolute genuineness; and the work which he had to perform in bringing them together, completing them and authenticating them was no light one.

A rather interesting story is told of the manner in which the King, when still little more than a child, acquired a taste for the science of numismatics. One day, he received a *soldo* bearing the head of Pope Pius IX, which he kept. A little later, finding another, he added it to the first; and, in this way, he ended by collecting fifteen. Meanwhile, his father, King Humbert, presented him with some sixty pieces of old copper money; and he thus formed the nucleus of his collection.

Thenceforward, at every anniversary, on his birthday, at Christmas, at Easter, the different members of the royal family, who used to chaff him about his new passion, gave him coins or medals. He made important purchases on his own account; and, finally, in 1900, he doubled the dimensions of his collection at one stroke by buying the inestimable treasure of coins belonging to the Marchese Marignoli, which was on the point of being dispersed to the four corners of the earth.

He admits, nevertheless, that the piece that represents the highest value in his eyes is a gold Montenegrin coin struck in the early days of the Petrovich dynasty and presented to him by Princess Helena of Montenegro at the time of their engagement. This coin is so rare that only one specimen is known to exist, apart from that in the possession of Victor Emanuel III; it is in the numismatical gallery at Vienna.

The King, moreover, has enriched his collection lately with an exceedingly rare series of coins of the Avignon popes. They were sold at auction at Frankfort; and a spirited contest took place between buyers acting respectively on behalf of King Victor Emanuel, the Pope and the director of our own gallery of medals.

It was, therefore, with a very special interest that he visited our mint, whose collection is famed throughout Europe. The director, knowing that he had to do with a connoisseur, had taken a great deal of trouble; in fact, I believe that he intended to "stagger" the King with his erudition. But he reckoned without his host, or rather his guest; and instead of the expert dazzling the King, it was the King who astonished the expert. He surprised him to such good purpose, with the accuracy and extent of his information on the subject of coins, that the learned director had to own himself beaten:

"We are school-boys beside Your Majesty," he confessed, in all humility.

And I think that this was something more than a courtier's phrase.

The King, as I have said, takes a keen interest in military matters. He displayed it on the occasion of the review of the Paris garrison. Even as he had appeared bored at the concert at the Élysée on the previous evening, so now he seemed to enjoy the impressive spectacle which we were able to offer him on the drill-ground at Vincennes. He wished to ride along the front of the troops on horse-back and had brought with him from Italy, for this purpose, his own saddle, a very handsome, richly-caparisoned, military saddle. The governor of Paris having lent him a charger, he proved himself a first-rate horseman, for the animal, unnerved at having to carry a harness heavier than that to which it was accustomed, could hit upon nothing better than to make a display of its ill-temper, regardless of the august quality of its rider. It was the worst day's work that that horse ever did in its life, and it had to recognise that it had found its master.

After making a thorough inspection of the troops by the side of the minister of war, the King expressed a desire to examine the outfit of one of the soldiers; and a private was ordered to fall out of the ranks. Victor Emanuel took up the soldier's knapsack, handled it, looked through it and made a movement as though to buckle it to the man's shoulders again himself, whereat the worthy little *pioupiou*, quite scared and red with dismay, cried:

"Oh, no, thanks, *mon—mon—*"

But the poor fellow, who had never even spoken to a general, had no notion how to address a king!

Thereupon the King, greatly amused, made a charming reply:

"Call me what your forebears, the French soldiers in 1859, called my grandfather on the night of the battle of Palestro; call me *mon caporal!*"

Victor Emanuel has too practical and matter-of-fact a mind to be what is known as a man of sentiment. Nevertheless, I saw him betray a real emotion when he was taken, on the following day, to visit the tomb of Napoleon I. The tomb was surrounded by six old pensioners carrying lighted torches. There were but few people there; the fitful flames of the torches cast their fantastic gleams upon the imperial sarcophagus; and the invisible presence of the Great Conqueror hovered over us: it seemed as though he would suddenly rise bodily out of that yawning gulf, that coffin of marble, dressed in his grey overcoat and his immemorial hat.

During a long silence, the King stood and dreamt, with bowed head. When we left the chapel, he was dreaming still.

I had another striking picture of Victor Emanuel III during the day's shooting with which M. Loubet provided him in the preserves at Rambouillet. The King, whose love of sport equals his passion for numismatics, is a first-rate shot. He aims at a great height, is careful of his cartridges and rarely misses a bird. According to custom, he was followed at Rambouillet by a keeper carrying a second gun, loaded, of course, in advance.

Now it happened that the King, seeing a flock of pheasants, began by discharging both barrels and bringing down a brace of birds. He then took the other gun, which the keeper held ready for him, put it to his shoulder and pulled the trigger; both shots missed fire. The keeper had forgotten to load the gun! Picture the rage of the sovereign, who, disconsolate at losing his pheasants, began to rate the culprit harshly! The unfortunate keeper, feeling more dead than alive, did not know what excuse to make; and he looked upon his place as fairly lost.

Then the King, guessing the man's unspoken fears, abruptly changed his tone:

"Never mind," he said. "There's no forgiving you; but I shall not say anything about it."

The King was obviously delighted with his day's sport. Yet, among the many attentions which we paid our guests during their brief stay in Paris, one surprise which we prepared for them was, if I am not mistaken, more acceptable to them—and especially to the Queen—than any other. This surprise consisted in the recital before Their Majesties, by our great actress, Madame Bartet, of the Comédie Française, of an unpublished poem from the pen of the Queen herself.

Helena of Montenegro had been a poet, in fact, in her leisure hours. At the time when she was engaged to be married, she wrote a poem in Russian which she sent to a St. Petersburg magazine, under the pseudonym of "Blue Butterfly"; and the magazine printed it without knowing the author's real name. It was written in rhythmical prose; and I was fortunate enough to procure a copy of the translation:

VISION

The mother said to her daughter:

"Wouldst know how the world is made? Open thine eyes."

And the little maid opened her eyes. She saw lordly and towering mountains, she saw valleys full of delights, she saw the sun which shines upon and gilds all things, she saw twinkling stars and the deep billows of the sea, she saw torrents with foaming waters and flowers with varied perfumes, she saw light-winged birds and the golden sheaves of the harvest. Then she closed her eyes.

And then she saw, she saw the fairest thing upon this earth: the image of the beloved who filled her heart, the image of the beloved who shone within her soul, the image of the beloved who gave his love in return for the love that was hers.

THE KING AND QUEEN OF ITALY AND THE CROWN PRINCE

This charming fragment had been recovered by a collector of royal poetry some time before the visit of the Italian sovereigns. M. André Rivoire, one of our finest poets, transposed it into French verse; and M. Loubet delicately caused it to be recited to our hosts in the course of a reception given in their honour at the Élysée. That evening, the beautiful Queen enjoyed a twofold success, as a woman and as a poetess.

5.

The unpretending affability of the royal couple was bound to win the affections of the French people. The daily more enthusiastic cheers that greeted them in their drives through Paris proved that they had conquered all hearts.

"It is astonishing," said an Italian official to me, "but they are even more popular here than at home!"

"That must be because they show themselves more," I replied.

At the risk of disappointing the reader, I am bound to confess that no tragic or even unpleasant incident came to spoil their pleasure or their peace of mind. It appeared that the anarchist gentry were allowing themselves a little holiday.

In the absence of the traditional plot, we had, it is true, the inevitable shower of anonymous letters and even some that were signed. The Queen, alas, had done much to encourage epistolary mendicants by announcing her wish that replies should be sent to all letters asking for assistance and that, in every possible case, satisfaction should be given to the writers. The result was that all the poverty-stricken Italians with whom Paris teems gave themselves free scope to their hearts' delight; and the usual fraternity of French begging-letter-writers—those who had formerly so artlessly striven to excite the compassion of the Shah of Persia—also tried what they could do.

But what reply was it possible to send to such letters as the following (I have kept a few specimens)?

"*To Her Majesty the Queen of Italy.*

"*Madame,*—

"We are a young married couple, honest, but poor. We were unable to have a honeymoon, for lack of money. It would be our dream to go to Italy, which is said to be the land of lovers. We thought that Your Majesty, loving your husband as you do and, therefore, knowing what love means, might consent to help us to make this little journey. We should want 500 francs; we entreat Your Majesty to lend it to us. When my husband has a better situation—he is at present an assistant in a curiosity-shop—he will not fail to repay Your Majesty the money.

"Pray accept the thanks, Madame, of

"Your Majesty's respectful and grateful servant,

"Marie G—,

"*Poste Restante 370,*

"Paris."

"*To His Majesty the King of Italy.*

"*Sir,—*

"I am a young painter full of ambition and said to be not devoid of talent. I am very anxious to see Rome and to study its artistic masterpieces. Not possessing the necessary means, I am writing to ask if you would not give me an employment of any kind, even in the service of the royal motor-cars (for I know how to drive a motor), so that I may be enabled in my spare time, to visit the monuments and picture-galleries and to perfect myself in my art.

"Pray accept, etc.

"Louis S—,

"*At the Café du Capitole,*

"Toulouse."

Here is a letter of another description:

"*To Her Majesty Queen Helena.*

"*Madame,—*

"You are the mother of two pretty babies: for this reason, I have the honour of sending you herewith two boxes of lacteal farinaceous food, of my own invention, for infants of tender years. It is a wonderful strengthening and tonic diet and I feel that I am doing Your Majesty a service in sending you these samples. You are sure to order more.

"In the hope of receiving these orders, I am,

"Your Majesty's respectful servant,

"Dr. F. J.,

"*Rue de la Liberté,*

"Nîmes."

These few specimens of correspondence will suffice to give an idea of the harmless and sometimes comical literature that found its way every morning into the royal letter-bag. I must not, however, omit to mention, among the humorous incidents that marked the sovereign's journey, an amusing mistake which occurred on the day of their arrival in Paris.

It was about half-past six in the evening. Our royal guests had that moment left the Foreign Office, to pay their first official visit to the President of the Republic, when a cab stopped outside the strictly-guarded gate. An old gentleman, very tall, with a long white beard and very simply dressed, alighted and was about to walk in with a confident step.

Three policemen rushed to prevent him:

"Stop!" they cried. "No one is allowed in here."

"Oh," said the stranger, "but I want to see the King of Italy!"

"And who may you be?"

"The King of the Belgians."

They refused to believe him. When he persisted, however, they went in search of an official, who at once came and proffered the most abject apologies. Picture the faces of the policemen!

The King and Queen of Italy stayed only three days in Paris, as I have said.

"We will come back again," the Queen promised, when she stepped into the train, radiant at the reception which had been given her.

They have not returned hitherto. True, they passed through France, in the following year, on their way to England. I made the journey with them; but, as on their first arrival at Modane, the blinds of their carriage were lowered. They remained down throughout the journey. Were the royal pair asleep? I never heard.

VI

GEORGE I, KING OF THE HELLENES

1.

In one of the drawers of my desk lies a bundle of letters which I preserve carefully, adding to it, from time to time, when a fresh letter arrives. They are written in a neat and dainty hand, almost a woman's hand; the paper is of a very ordinary quality and bears no crown nor monogram; and the emblem stamped on the red wax with which the envelopes are sealed looks as though it had been selected on purpose to baffle indiscreet curiosity: it represents a head of Minerva wearing her helmet.

And yet this correspondence is very interesting; and I believe that an historian would attach great value to it, not only because it would supply him with nice particulars concerning certain events of our own time, but also because it reveals the exquisite feeling of one of the most attractive of sovereigns, the youthfulness of his mind and the reasons why a royal crown may sometimes seem heavy even under the radiant skies of Greece.

It is nearly twenty years since I first met the writer of those letters, the King of the Hellenes; and, since then, I have watched over his safety on the occasion of most of his visits to France. This long acquaintance enabled me to win his gracious kindness, while he has gained my affectionate devotion. I often take the liberty of writing to him, when he is in his own dominions; he never fails to reply with regularity; and our correspondence forms, as it were, a sequel to our familiar talks, full of good-humour and charm, begun at Aix-les-Bains, in Paris, or in the train.

It would be puerile to state that King George loves France; the frequency of his visits makes the fact too obvious. He does more than evince a warm admiration for our country: this Danish prince, who has worn the Greek crown for more than forty-six years, is, with his brother-in-law, King Edward VII, the most Parisian of our foreign guests. His Parisianism shows itself not only in the elegant ease with which he speaks our language: it is seen in his turn of mind, which is essentially that of the man about town, and in his figure, which is slender and strong, tall and graceful, like that of one of our cavalry-officers. The quick shrewdness that lurks behind his fair, military moustache is also peculiarly French; and the touch of fun which is emphasised by a constant twitching of the eyes and lips and which finds an outlet in felicitous phrases and unexpected sallies is just of the sort that makes people say of *us* that we are the most satirical people on the face of the earth.

King George's "fun," at any rate, is never cruel; and, if his chaff sometimes becomes a little caustic, at least it is always, if I may say so, to the point.

For instance, at the commencement of his reign, when he found himself grappling with the first internal difficulties, one of the leaders of the parliamentary opposition, which was very anxious for the fall of the ministry so that it might itself take office, came to him and said, with false and deceitful melancholy:

"Ah, Sir, if you only had a minister!"

"A minister?" replied the King, with feigned surprise. "Why, I have seven at least!"

The King was brought up in the admirable school of simplicity, rectitude and kindness of his father, King Christian, and was made familiar, from his early youth, with all the tortuous paths of the political maze. When the fall of King Otho placed him, by the greatest of accidents, on the throne of Greece, he brought with him not only the influence of his numberless illustrious alliances and the fruits of a timely experience gained in that marvellous observation-post which the Court of Denmark supplies: he also brought the qualities of his cold and well-balanced northern temperament to that people which does not require the stimulation of its Patras wine to become hot-headed.

And what difficult times the King has passed through!

The King of Saxony, visiting Corfu one day, said to him, the next morning:

"Upon my word, it must be charming to be king of this paradise!"

"You must never repeat that wish," replied King George, without hesitation. "I have been its king for thirty years; and speak as one who knows!"

Events that have followed since have amply justified the bitterness of this outburst, which I find renewed in the sovereign's letters. And yet, grave as the Greek crisis is at the moment of writing, I do not believe that the crown is in any danger. The Greeks, without distinction of party, recognise the great services their ruler has rendered to the national cause, which he has defended for the past ten years in the European *chancelleries* with indefatigable zeal and eloquence.

"I never met a more persuasive or more able diplomat," said M. Clémenceau, last year after a visit which he received from George I.

His ability has not only consisted in defending his country against the ambitious projects of Turkey by placing her under the protection of the powers interested in preserving the *status quo* in the East; it has been shown in the ease with which he effects his ends amid the party quarrels that envenom political life in Greece. Guided by his native common-sense and a remarkable knowledge of mankind, he has made it his study, in governing, to let people do and say what they please, at least to an extent that enables him never to find himself in open opposition to the love of independence and the easily-offended pride of his subjects; he has realised that what was required was an uncommon readiness to yield, rather than inflexible principles; and, of all the ministers who succeeded one another since his accession, the celebrated Coumandouros appears to be the one from whom His Majesty derived and retained the best system of ironical, easy-going government.

For the rest, it must be admitted that, although the Greek nation is sometimes tiresome, with its faults and weaknesses which, for that matter, are purely racial and temperamental, on the other hand it is generous and impulsive to a degree; and its touchy pride is only the effect of an ardent patriotism which is sometimes manifested in the most amusing ways.

For instance, when Greece, not long ago, revived an ancient and picturesque tradition and decided to restore the Olympic Games and when it became evident that these would draw large numbers of foreigners to Athens, the pickpockets held a meeting and pledged themselves one and all to suspend hostilities as long as the games lasted, in order to guard the reputation of the country. They even took care to inform the public of the resolution which they had passed; and they did more; they kept their word, with this unprecedented result, that the police had a holiday, thanks to the strike of the thieves!

Last year, Mme. Jacquemaire, a daughter of M. Clémenceau, then prime minister of France, made a journey to Greece. Returning by rail from Athens to the Piræus, where she was to take ship for Trieste, she missed her travelling-bag, containing her jewels. This valuable piece of luggage had evidently been stolen; and she lost no time in lodging a complaint with the harbour-police, although she was convinced of the uselessness of the step. The quest instituted was, in fact, vain. But meanwhile the press had seized upon the incident and stirred up public opinion, which was at that time persuaded that M. Clémenceau, whose Philhellenic leanings are notorious, had promised the Greek government his support in its efforts to obtain the annexation of Crete. The daughter of the man upon whom the Greeks based such hopes as these must not, people said, be allowed to take an unfavourable impression of Greek hospitality away with her. The newspapers published strongly-worded articles entreating the unknown thief, if he was a Greek, to give up the profit of his larceny and to perform a noble and unselfish act; placards posted on the walls of Athens and the Piræus made vehement appeals to his patriotism. Twenty-four hours later, the police received the bag and its contents untouched; and they were restored to Mme. Jacquemaire on her arrival at Trieste.

2.

The pilot's trade is a hard one when you have to steer through continual rocks, to keep a constant eye upon a turbulent crew and to look out for the "squalls" which are perpetually beating down from the always stormy horizon in the East. It is easily understood that King George should feel a longing, when events permit, to go to other climes in search of a short diversion from his absorbing responsibilities.

"You see," said King Leopold of the Belgians to me one day, "our real rest lies in forgetting *who* we are."

And yet it cannot be said the distractions and the rest which King George knew that he would find among us were the only object of the journeys across Europe which he made every year until the year before last. He always carried a diplomatist's dispatch-box among his luggage; he is one of those who believe that a sovereign can travel for his country while travelling for pleasure.

"I am my own ambassador," he often said to me.

The King used to come to us generally at the beginning of the autumn, on his way to and from Copenhagen, where he never omitted to visit his father, King Christian, and his sisters, Queen Alexandra and the Empress Marie Feodorovna. He delighted in this annual gathering, which collected round the venerable grandsire under the tall trees of Fredensborg, the largest and most illustrious family that the world contains, a family over which the old king's ascendancy and authority remained so great that his children, were they emperors or kings, dared not go into Copenhagen without first asking his leave.

"When I am down there, I feel as if I were still a little boy," King George used to say, laughing.

In France, he was a young man. He divided his stay between Aix-les-Bains and Paris; and in Paris, as at Aix, he had but one thought in his head: to avoid all official pomp and ceremony. He would have been greatly distressed if he had been treated too obviously as a sovereign; and, when he accepted the inevitable official dinner to which the President of the Republic always invited him, he positively refused the royal salute. When at Aix, he used to yield to the necessity of attending the festivities which the authorities of that charming watering-place, where he was very popular, arranged in his honour; but only because he did not wish to wound anyone's feelings, however slightly. And, when invited to go to some display of fireworks:

"Come!" he would sigh. "Another party in my honour!"

Other business detained me and I had not the privilege of being attached to his person during his first stay at Aix. The French Government sent two commissioners from Lyons to watch over his safety; and these worthy functionaries, who had never been charged with a mission of this kind before, lived in a continual state of alarm. To them, guarding a king meant never to lose sight of him, to follow him step by step like a prisoner, to spy upon his movements as though he were a felon. They ended by driving our guest mad: no sooner had he left his bed-room than two shadows fastened on to his heels and never quitted him; if he went to a restaurant, to the casino, to the theatre, two stern, motionless faces appeared in front of him, four suspicious eyes peered into his least action. It was of no avail for him to try to throw the myrmidons off the scent, to look for back-doors by which to escape from them: there was no avoiding them; they were always there. He made a discreet complaint and I was asked to replace them.

"You are very welcome," he said, when I arrived. "Your colleagues from Lyons made such an impression on me that I ended by taking myself for an assassin!"

To my mind the mission of guarding this particularly unaffected and affable King was neither a very absorbing nor a very thankless task. At Aix, where he walked about from morning to night like any ordinary private person, everybody knew him. There was never the least need for me to consult the reports of my inspectors; the saunterers, the shopkeepers, the peasants made it their business to keep me informed.

"Monsieur le Roi," they would say, "has just passed this way; he went down that turning."

Then I would see a familiar form twenty yards ahead, stick in hand, Homburg hat on one ear, the slim, brisk figure clad in a light grey suit, strolling down the street, or looking into a shop-window, or stopping in the midst of a group of workmen. It was "Monsieur le Roi."

KING GEORGE OF GREECE IN THE STREETS OF PARIS

"Monsieur le Roi" had even become "Monsieur Georges" to the pretty laundresses whom he greeted with a pleasant "Good-morning" when he passed them at the wash-tubs on his way to the bathing establishment. For he carefully followed the cure of baths and douches which his trusty physician, Dr. Guillard, prescribed for his arthritis. He left the hotel early every morning and walked to the Baths, taking a road that leads through one of the oldest parts of Aix. The inhabitants of that picturesque corner came to know him so well by sight that they ended by treating him as a friendly neighbour. Whenever he entered the Rue du Puits-d'Enfer, the street-boys would stop playing and receive him with merry cheers, to which he replied by flinging handfuls of coppers to them. The news of his approach flew from door to door till it reached the laundry. Forthwith, the girls stopped the rhythmic beat of their "dollies"; the songs ceased on their lips; they quickly wiped the lather from their hands on a corner of the skirt or apron and came out of doors, while their fresh young voices gave him the familiar greeting:

"Good-morning, M. Georges! Three cheers for M. Georges!"

They chatted for a bit; the King amused himself by asking questions, joking, replying; then, touching the brim of his felt hat, he went his way with the bright voices calling after him prettily:

"Au revoir, M. Georges! Till to-morrow!"

He enjoyed this morning call before getting into the "deep bath" reserved for him; and he himself was popular in and around the laundry in the Rue du Puits-d'Enfer, not only because of his good-nature and good-humour, but because the girls had more than once experienced the benefits of his unobtrusive generosity.

His days, at Aix as in Paris, were regulated with mathematical precision: George I is a living chronometer! After making his daily pilgrimage to the Baths, he returned to the hotel, read his telegrams, dipped into the French and English newspapers and worked with his Master of the Household, Count Cernovitz, or with his equerry, General de Reineck, or else with M. Delyanni, the deeply-regretted Greek minister to Paris, whom he honoured with a great affection and who always joined his royal master at Aix.

From eleven to twelve in the morning, he generally gave audiences, either to the authorities of Aix, with whom he maintained cordial relations, or to strangers of note who were presented to him during his stay. When he kept a few people to lunch—which often happened—they had to resign themselves to leaving their appetite unsatisfied. The King eats very little in the day-time and not only ordered a desperately frugal *menu*, but himself touched nothing except the *hors-d'œuvre*. His visitors naturally thought themselves obliged, out of deference to imitate his example, the more so as, otherwise, they ran the risk of having their mouths full at the moment when they had to reply to the King's frequent questions. His regular guests, therefore, the prefect and the mayor, knowing by experience what was in store for them, had adopted a system which was both practical and ingenious: whenever they were invited to the royal table they lunched before they came.

In the evening, on the other hand, His Majesty made a hearty meal. He always dined in the public room of the restaurant of the Casino, with his medical adviser and some friends; and, when Dr. Guillard cried out against the excessive number of courses which the royal host was fond of ordering:

"Don't be angry with me," he replied. "I don't order them for myself, but for the good of the house; if the restaurant didn't make a profit out of me, where would it be?"

After dinner, he took us with him either to the gaming-rooms or to the theatre. Although the King did not play himself, it amused him to stroll round the tables, to watch the expression of the gamblers, and to observe the numberless typical incidents that always occur among such a cosmopolitan crowd as that consisting of the frequenters of our watering-places. He also loved to hear the gossip of the place, to know all about the petty intrigues, the little domestic tragedies. Lastly, he liked making the acquaintance of any well-known actor or actress who happened to be passing through Aix.

One evening, seeing Mlle. Balthy, the famous comic reciter, at the Casino and knowing, by hearsay, what a witty woman she was, he told me that he would be glad to meet her; and nothing was easier than to satisfy the King's wish. Nevertheless, the idea frightened me a little: the humour of the charmingly eccentric artist that Balthy is, sometimes adopts so very daring a form, and I dreaded lest her remarks might be a little too "startling." I spoke my mind on the subject to the King.

"Never fear, Paoli," he said. "Mlle. Balthy's 'startling' side will amuse me immensely: you need not be a greater royalist than the King!"

So I went in search of the delightful creature:

"My dear Balthy," I said, "come with me and be presented to the King."

"To George?" she replied, winking her eye.

I shuddered with dismay!

"To His Majesty the King of the Hellenes, yes."

"Come on!"

But lo and behold, in the King's presence, Balthy—O, wonder of wonders!—lost all her self-assurance. I expected to see her tap the King on the shoulder; instead, she made him an elaborate curtsey. In reply to the compliments which he paid her she was content modestly to lower her eyes: she even went so far as to blush! We might have been at court.

And, when the King, not knowing what to think, and feeling perhaps a trifle disappointed, confessed his surprise at her shyness:

"What can you expect?" she declared. "If even you were merely a president of the republic, it wouldn't put me out; but a king—that makes me feel uncomfortable! And, besides, no king can care for thin women; and I should look like a sardine, even if you put me next to Sarah Bernhardt!"

The ice was broken. The Balthy of tradition began to peep through the surface and the King was delighted.

Our guest did more than show his liking for the shining light of the profession: he numbered friends also among the humble performers at the Grand Théâtre. Sabadon, the good, jolly, indescribable Sabadon, who for twenty years had sung first "heavy bass" at the theatre of the town, was one of them. This is how I discovered the fact: when the King came to Aix, some years ago, Sabadon shouldered his way to the front row of the spectators who were waiting outside the station to see His Majesty arrive. The enthusiastic crowd kept on shouting, "Long live King George!" and Sabadon, with his powerful voice, his "heavy bass" voice, which had filled all the "grand theatres" in the provinces, Sabadon, with his southern accent (he was from Toulouse) shouted louder than all the rest and, so that he might shout more freely, had taken a step forward.

But a policeman was watching; and fearing lest the royal procession should be disturbed by this intrusive person, he walked up to him and, in a bullying tone, said:

"Get back; and look sharp about it. You don't imagine you're going to stand in the King's road, do you?"

Sabadon, who is a hot-blooded fellow, like all the men from his part of the country, was about to reply with one of those forcible and pungent outbursts which are the salt of the Gascon speech:

"You low, rascally—" he began.

But he had no time to finish. The King appeared at the entrance to the railway-station, came across and, as he passed, said:

"Hullo, M. Sabadon! How do you do, M. Sabadon? Are they biting this year?"

"Yes, Sir, Your Majesty. And your family? Keeping well, I hope? That's right!"

Then, when the King had disappeared, Sabadon turned to the astounded policeman:

"What do you say to that, my son? Flabbergasts you, eh?"

How did the King come to know the singer? And why had he asked with so much interest if "they were biting this year"? One of the local papers reported the incident and supplied the explanation, which I did not trouble to verify, but which is so amusing and, at the same time, probable that I give it here. The King, it seems, who often walked to the Lac du Bourget, a few miles from Aix, thought that he would try his hand at fishing, one afternoon. Taking the necessary tackle with him, he sat down on the shore of the lake and cast his line. Ten minutes, twenty minutes passed. Not a bite. The King felt the more annoyed as, thirty yards from where he was, a man—a stranger like himself—was pulling up his line at every moment with a trout or a bream wriggling at the end of it.

The disheartened King ended by deciding to go up to the angler and ask him how he managed to catch so many fish! But before he was able to say a word, the man stood up, bowed with great ceremony and, in a stentorian voice, said:

"Sir, Your Majesty...."

"What! Do you know me?" asked the King.

"Sir, Your Majesty, let me introduce myself: Sabadon, second heavy bass at the Théâtre du Capitole of Toulouse, at this moment first chorus-leader at the Théâtre Municipal of Aix-les-Bains. I have seen you in the stage-box."

"Ah!" said the King, taken aback. "But please explain to me why you get so many fish, whereas...."

"Habit, Sir, Your Majesty, a trick of the hand and personal fascination; it needs an education; I got mine at Pinsaquel, near Toulouse, at the junction of the Ariège and the Gavonne.... Ah, Pinsaquel!"

And Sabadon's voice was filled with all the pangs of homesickness:

"Have you never been to Pinsaquel? You ought to go; it's the anglers' paradise."

"Certainly, I will go there one day. But, meanwhile, I shall be returning with an empty basket."

"Never, not if I know it! Take my place, Sir, Your Majesty, each time I say 'Hop'! pull up your line, and tell me what you think of it!"

The King, mightily amused by the adventure, followed his instructions. In three minutes Sabadon's tremendous voice gave the signal:

"Hop!"

It was a trout. And the fishing went on, in an almost miraculous manner.

As they walked back to the town together, an hour later, Sabadon took the opportunity to expound to the King the cause of his grudge against Meyerbeer, the composer:

"You must understand, Sir, Your Majesty, that, at the theatre, at Toulouse, it was I who used to play the night watchman in the *Huguenots*. I had to cross the stage with a lantern; and, as I am very popular at Toulouse, I used to receive a wonderful ovation: "Bravo, Sabadon! Hurrah for Sabadon!" Just as when you came to Aix, Sir, Your Majesty.... Well, in spite of that the manager absolutely refused to let me take a call, because the music didn't lend itself to it! I ask you, Sir, Your Majesty, if that lout of a Meyerbeer couldn't have let me cross the stage a second time!"

3.

King George, who, like most reigning sovereigns, is an indefatigable walker, used to start out every day in the late afternoon and come back just before dinner-time. He nearly always took a member of his suite with him; one of my inspectors would follow him. All the peasants round Aix knew the King by sight and raised their caps as he passed. He is very young in mind—in this respect, he has remained the midshipman of his boyhood—and he sometimes amused himself by playing a trick on the companion of his walk. For instance, as soon as he saw that his equerry, after covering a reasonable number of miles, was beginning, if I may so express myself, to hang out signals of distress, the King suggested that they should turn into a roadside public-house for a drink.

"They keep a certain small wine of the country here," he said, "which has a flavour all of its own; but you must drink it down at a draught."

The other, whether he was thirsty or not, dared not refuse. They therefore entered the inn and the King had a tumbler filled with the famous nectar and handed it to his equerry, taking good care not to drink any himself. It was, in point of fact, a *piquette*, or sour wine, with a taste "all of its own" and resembling nothing so much as vinegar; and the King's guest, when he had emptied his glass, could not help pulling a frightful face. He dared not, however, be so disrespectful as to complain; and when the King, who had enjoyed the scene enormously, asked, in a very serious voice:

"Delicious, isn't it?"

"Oh, delicious!" the equerry replied, with an air of conviction.

You must not, however, think that the King's practical jokes were always cruel. Most often, they bore witness, under a superficial appearance of mischief, to his discriminating kindness of heart.

I remember, in this connexion, once going to meet him at the frontier-station of Culoz, through which he was passing on his way from Geneva to Aix. The members of his suite and I had left him alone, for a few moments, while we went to buy some books and newspapers which he had asked for. As he was walking up and down the platform, he saw a good woman at the door of a third-class railway-carriage, a plump, red-faced sort of peasant-woman, who was making vain efforts to open the door and fuming with anger and impatience. Suddenly catching sight of the King, who stood looking at her:

"Hi, there, Mr. Porter!" she cried. "Come and help me, can't you?"

The King ran up, opened the carriage-door and received the fat person in his arms. Next, she said:

"Fetch me out my basket of vegetables and my bundle."

The King obediently executed her commands. At that moment we appeared upon the platform, and to our amazement saw King George carrying the basket under one arm and the bundle under the other. He made a sign to me not to move. He carried the luggage to the waiting-room, took a ticket for the fair traveller, who was changing her train, and refused to accept payment for it, in spite of her insistence. What a pleasant recollection she must have of the porters at Culoz Station!

Here is another adventure, which happened at Aix. The King had the habit, on leaving the Casino in the evening, to go back with me in the hotel-omnibus, which was reserved for his use: he found this easier than taking a cab. One evening, just as we were about to step in, a visitor staying at the hotel, a foreign lady, not knowing that the omnibus was reserved exclusively for the King, went in before us, sat down and waited for the 'bus to start. As I was about to ask her to get out:

"Let her be," said the King. "She's not in our way."

We got inside in our turn; I sat down opposite the King; the omnibus started; the lady did not move. Suddenly, the King broke silence and spoke to me; I replied, using, of course, the customary forms of "Sire" and "Your Majesty."

Thereupon the lady looked at us in dismay, flung herself against the window, tapped at it, called out:

"What have I done? Heavens, what have I done?" she cried. "I am in the King's omnibus! Stop! Stop!"

And turning to the King, with a theatrical gesture:

"Pardon, Sire."

The King was seized with a fit of laughing, in the midst of which he did his best to reassure her:

"I entreat you, Madam, calm yourself! You have nothing to fear: a King is not an epidemic disease!"

The good lady quieted down; but we reached the hotel without being able to extract a word from her paralysed throat.

In this respect, she did not resemble the majority of her sisters of the fair sex, before whose imperious and charming despotism we have bowed since the days of our father Adam. As a matter of fact, no sovereign that I know of ever aroused more affectionate curiosity in the female circles than King George. The glamour of his rank had something to say to the matter, no doubt; but I have reason to believe that the elegance of his person, the affability of his manners and the conquering air of his moustache were not wholly unconnected with it. Whether leaving his hotel, or entering the restaurant or one of the rooms of the Casino, or appearing in the paddock at the races, which he attended regularly, he became the cynosure of every pair of bright eyes and the object of cunning manœuvres on the part of their pretty owners, who were anxious to approach him and to find out what a king is made of when you see him close. No man is quite insensible to such advances. At the same time, George I was too clever to be taken in; he was amused at the homage paid him and accepted it in his usual spirit of bantering, but polite coyness, although the ladies' persistence often became both indiscreet and troublesome.

For the rest, he led a very quiet, very methodical and rather monotonous life, both at Aix and in Paris; for to the character of this sovereign, as to that of most others, there is a "middle-class" side that displays itself in harmless eccentricities. For instance, King George, when he travels abroad, always goes to the same hotel, occupies the same rooms and is so averse to change that he likes every piece of furniture to be in exactly the same place where he last left it. I shall never forget my astonishment when, entering the King's bed-room a few moments after his arrival at the Hôtel Bristol in Paris, I caught him bodily moving a heavy Louis-XV chest of drawers, which he carried across the room with the help of his physician.

"You see," he said, "it used to stand by the fireplace and they have shifted it to the window, so I am putting it back."

Certainly, he had the most wonderful memory for places that I ever observed.

4.

I have spoken of my duties with regard to this monarch as an agreeable sinecure. But I was exaggerating. Once, when I was with him at Aix, I had a terrible alarm. I was standing beside him, in the evening, in the *petits-chevaux* room at the Casino, when one of my inspectors slipped a note into my hand. It was to inform me that an individual of Roumanian nationality, a rabid Grecophobe, had arrived at Aix, with, it was feared, the intention of killing the King. There was no further clue.

I was in a very unpleasant predicament. I did not like to tell the King, for fear of spoiling his stay. To go just then in search of further details would have been worse still: there could be no question of leaving the King alone. How could I discover the man? For all I knew, he was quite near; and instinctively, I scrutinised carefully all the people who crowded round us, kept my eyes fixed on those who seemed to be staring too persistently at the King and watched every movement of the players.

At daybreak the next morning, I set to work and started enquiries. I had no difficulty in discovering my man. He was a Roumanian student and had put up at a cheap hotel; he was said to be rather excitable in his manner, if not in his language. I could not arrest him as long as I had no definite charge brought against him. I resolved to have him closely shadowed by the Aix police and I myself arranged never to stir a foot from the King's side. Things went on like this for several days: the King knew nothing and the Roumanian neither; but I would gladly have bought him a railway-ticket to get rid of him.

Presently, however, one of my inspectors came to me, wearing a terrified look:

"We've lost the track of the Roumanian!" he declared.

"You are mad!" I cried.

"No, would I were! He has left his hotel unnoticed by any of us; and we don't know what has become of him."

I flew into a rage and at once ordered a search to be made for him. It was labour lost; there was not a trace of him to be found.

For once, I was seriously uneasy. I resolved to tell the whole story to the King so that he might allow himself to be quietly guarded. But he merely shrugged his shoulders and laughed.

"You see, Paoli," he said, "I am a fatalist. If my hour has come, neither you nor I can avoid it; and I am certainly not going to let a trifle of this kind spoil my holiday. Besides, it is not the first time that I have seen danger close at hand; and I assure you that I am not afraid. Look here, a few years ago, I was returning one day with my daughter to my castle of Tatoï, near Athens. We were driving, without an escort. Suddenly, happening to turn my head, I saw a rifle barrel pointed at us from the road side, gleaming between the leaves of the bushes. I leaped up and instantly flung myself in front of my daughter. The rifle followed me. I said to myself, 'It's all over; I'm a dead man.' And what do you think I did? I have never been able to explain why, but I began to count aloud—'One, two, three'—it seemed an age; and I was just going to say, 'Four,' when the shot was fired. I closed my eyes. The bullet whistled past my ears. The startled horses ran away, we were saved and I thought no more about it. So do not let us alarm ourselves before the event, my dear Paoli: we will wait and see what happens."

I admired the King's fine coolness, of course; but I was none the easier in my mind for all that. Still, the King was right, this time, and I was wrong: we never heard anything more about the mysterious Roumanian.

5.

George I has preserved none but agreeable recollections of his different visits to Aix. In evidence of this, I will only mention the regret which he expressed to me, in one of his last letters, that the Greek crisis prevented him from making his usual trip to France in 1909:

"Here where duty keeps me—nobody knows for how long—I often think of my friends at Aix, of my friends in France, whom I should so much like to see again; of that beautiful country, of our walks and talks. But life is made up of little sacrifices; they do not count, if we succeed in attaining the object which we pursue; and mine is to ensure for my people the happiness which they deserve."

The King has depicted his very self in those few words: I know no better portrait of him.

VII

QUEEN WILHELMINA OF THE NETHERLANDS

1.

I had the honour of presenting myself in person to Queen Wilhelmina on the first of November, 1895, at Geneva, the city where, a year earlier, I had gone to meet the tragic and charming Empress Elizabeth of Austria and where, three years later, I was fated to see her lying on a bed in an hotel, stabbed to death. The official instructions with which I was furnished stated that I was to accompany their Majesties the Queen and Queen Regent of the Netherlands from Geneva to Aix-les-Bains and to ensure their safety during their stay on French soil.

I have preserved a pleasant recollection of this presentation, which took place on the station-platform on a dull, wintry morning. I remember how, while I was introducing myself to General Du Monceau, the Queen's principal aide-de-camp, there suddenly appeared on the foot-board of the royal carriage a young girl with laughing eyes, her face agleam and pink under her flaxen tresses, very simply dressed in a blue tailor-made skirt and coat, with a big black boa round her neck. And I remember a fresh, almost childish voice that made the general give a brisk half-turn and a courtly bow.

"General," she said, "don't forget to buy me some post cards!"

This pink, fair-haired girl, with the clear voice, was Queen Wilhelmina, who at that time was the very personification of the title of "the little Queen" which Europe, with one accord, had bestowed upon her, a title suggestive of fragile grace, touching familiarity and affectionate deference. She was just sixteen years of age. It was true that, as a poet had written:

A pair of woman's eyes already gazed
Above her childish smile;

and that her apprenticeship in the performance of a queen's duties had already endowed her mind with a precocious maturity. Nevertheless, her ready astonishment, her spontaneity, her frank gaiety, her reckless courage showed that she was still a real girl, in the full sense of the word. She hastened, happy and trusting, to the encounter of life; she blossomed like the tulips of her own far fields; she was of the age that gives imperious orders to destiny, that lives in a palace of glass! I doubt whether she really understood—although she never made a remark to me on the subject—that the French government had thought itself obliged to appoint a solemn functionary—even though it were only M. Paoli!—whose one and only mission was to protect her against the dagger of a possible assassin. The sweet little Queen could not imagine herself to possess an enemy; and the people who had approached her hitherto had learnt nothing from her but her gentle kindness.

As for Queen Emma, she was as simple and as easy of access as her daughter, although more reserved. She fulfilled her double task as regent and mother, as counsellor and educator with great dignity, bringing to it the virile authority, the spirit of decision and the equability of character which we so often find in women summoned by a too-early widowhood to assume the responsibilities of the head of a family. And nothing more edifying was ever seen than the close union that prevailed between those two illustrious ladies, who never left each other's side, taking all their meals alone, although they were accompanied by a numerous suite, and living in a constant communion of thought and in the still enjoyment of a mutual and most touching affection.

Their suite, as I have said, was a numerous one. In fact, it consisted, in addition to Lieutenant-General Count Du Monceau, of two chamberlains: Colonel (now Major-general) Jonkheer Willem van de Poll and Jonkheer Rudolph van Pabst van Bingerden (now Baron van Pabst van Bingerden); a business secretary: Jonkheer P. J. Vegelin van Claerbergen; two ladies-in-waiting: "Mesdemoiselles les baronnes" (as they were styled in the Dutch protocol) Elizabeth van Ittersum and Anna Juckema van Burmania Rengers; a reader: Miss Kreusler; five waiting-women; and five footmen. Compared with the tiny courts that usually accompanied other sovereigns when travelling, this made a somewhat imposing display! Nevertheless and notwithstanding the fact that this sixteen-year-old Queen appeared to me decked with the glory of a fairy princess, I am bound to admit that the royal circle presented none of the venerable austerity and superannuated grace so quaintly conjured up in Perrault's Tales. The Jonkheers[4] were not old lords equipped with shirt frills and snuff-boxes; *Mesdemoiselles les baronnes* were not severe duennas encased in stiff silk gowns: the court was young and gay, with that serene and healthy gaiety which characterises the Dutch temperament.

QUEEN WILHELMINA

Why was it going to Aix? The choice of this stay puzzled me. Aix-les-Bains is hardly ever visited in November. The principal hotels are closed, for, in that mountainous region, winter sets in with full severity immediately after the end of autumn.

I put the question to General Du Monceau, who explained to me that the doctors had recommended Queen Wilhelmina to take a three-week's cure of pure, keen air; and that was why they had selected Aix, or rather the Corbières, a spot situated at 2,000 feet above Aix, on the slope of the Grand Revard.

It goes without saying that there was no hotel there; and the only villa in the neighbourhood had to be hired for the Queens' use. This was a large wooden chalet, standing at the skirt of a pine-forest, close to the hamlet. The wintry wind whistled under the doors and howled down the chimneys; there was no central heating-apparatus and huge fires were lit in every room. From the windows of this rustic dwelling, the eye took in the amphitheatre of the mountains of Savoy and their deep and beautiful valleys; and, above the thatched roofs ensconced among the trees, one saw little columns of blue smoke rise trembling to the sky.

Snow began to fall on the day after our arrival. It soon covered the mountains all around with a cloak of dazzling white, spread a soft carpet over the meadows before the house and powdered the long tresses of the pines with hoar-frost. A great silence ensued; I seemed to be living more and more in the midst of a fairy-tale.

The court settled down as best it could. The two Queens occupied three unpretending rooms on the first floor; the royal suite divided the other apartments among them; some of the servants were lodged in a neighbouring farm-house. As for myself, I was bound to keep in daily telegraphic touch with Paris and with the prefect of the department; and I found it more convenient to sleep at Aix. I went up to the Corbières every morning by the funicular railway, which had been reopened for the use of our royal guests, and went down again, every evening, by the same route.

The two Queens, who appeared to revel in this stern solitude, had planned out for themselves a regular and methodical mode of life. They were up by eight o'clock in the morning and walked to the hamlet, chatted with the peasants and cowherds and, after a short stroll, returned to the villa, where Queen Emma, who, at that period, was still exercising the functions of regent, dispatched her affairs of State, while little Queen Wilhelmina employed her time in studying or drawing, for she was a charming and gifted draughtswoman. She loved nothing more than to jot down from life, so to speak, such rustic scenes as offered: peasant-lads leading their cows to the fields, or girls knitting or sewing on the threshold of their doors. The people round about came to know of this; they also knew that Her Majesty was in the habit of generously rewarding her willing models. And so, as soon as she had installed herself by the roadside, or in her garden, with her sketch-book and pencils, cows or little pigs accompanied by their owners, would spring up as though by magic!

I have said that the Queens were in the habit of taking their meals alone. Nevertheless, outside meals, they mingled very readily with the members of their suite, whom they honoured with an affectionate familiarity.

The afternoons—whatever the weather might be—were devoted to long walks, on which Queen Wilhelmina used to set out accompanied generally by one or two ladies-in-waiting and a chamberlain; sometimes I would go with her myself. Queen Emma, knowing her daughter's indefatigable venturesomeness, had given up accompanying her on her expeditions. We often returned covered with snow, our faces blue with the cold, our boots soaked through; but it made no difference; the little Queen was delighted. She dusted her gaiters, shook her skirt and her pale golden hair that hung over her shoulders and said:

"I wish it were to-morrow and that we were starting out again!"

2.

Queen Wilhelmina was very expansive in her manner and yet very thoughtful. Brought up in the strictest principles by a watchful and inflexible mother, she had learnt from childhood to shirk neither work nor fatigue, to brave the inclemencies of the weather, to distinguish herself alike in bodily and in mental exercises, in short, to prepare herself in the most serious fashion for her duties as Queen and to realise all the hopes that were centred on her young head.

I often had occasion, during my stay at the Corbières, to notice the thoroughness of her education. She already spoke four languages, in addition to her mother-tongue, fluently: French, Russian, English and German. She interested herself in agricultural matters and was not unacquainted with social questions: for instance, she often made me talk to her about the condition of the workmen in France and the organisation of our administrative systems; nay, more, she was beginning to study both judicial and constitutional law. I would not, however, go so far as to say that this study aroused her enthusiasm: she preferred I believe, to read historical books; she took a great interest in the Napoleonic idyll and, knowing me to be a fellow-countryman of Bonaparte:

"You must feel very sorry," she said to me, one day, "that you came too late to have seen him!"

She also liked to talk to me about her ponies:

"I have four," she told me, "and I drive them four-in-hand."

I was often invited to share the meals of the miniature court and to take my seat at the table of the chamberlains and ladies-in-waiting, which was presided over, with charming courtesy and geniality, by my excellent friend Count Du Monceau, who, although a Dutch general, was of French origin, as his name shows.[5]

At one of these dinners, I met with a little mishap which gave a great shock to both my patriotism and to my natural greediness. The cook of the villa, M. Perreard, was a native of Marseilles and owned an hotel at Cannes, where I had made his acquaintance. In his twofold capacity as a Marseillese and a cook, he was a great hand at making bouillabaisse, the national dish of the people of the south. Now, as he knew that I was very fond of this dainty, he said to me one day, with a great air of mystery:

"M. Paoli, I have a pleasant surprise in store for you at lunch this morning. I have sent to Marseilles for fish and shell-fish so as to give you a bouillabaisse cooked in the way you know of. Not another word! But they'll have a good time up there, I can tell you, those people from the north who have never tasted it!"

As soon as we had sat down, I saw with delight the great soup-tureen, whence escaped a delicious fragrance of bouillabaisse. The members of the royal suite cast inquisitive glances at this dish unknown to them and prepared to do honour to it with a good grace. Before tasting it myself, I watched the expression of their faces. Alas, a grievous disappointment awaited me! Hardly had they touched their spoons with their lips, when they gave vent to their disgust in different ways. Baroness van Ittersum made a significant grimace, while Jonkheer van Pabst pushed away his plate and Baroness Rengers suppressed a gesture of repugnance.

However, out of consideration for my feelings, they were silent: so was I. They waited in all kindness for me to enjoy my treat; but one act of politeness deserves another; there was nothing for me to do, in my turn, but to forego my share, all the more so as I did not feel inclined to present the ridiculous spectacle of a man eating by himself a thing which all his neighbours loathe and detest.

The bouillabaisse, therefore, disappeared straightway, untouched and still steaming, beating, as it were, a silent retreat. But I will not attempt to describe the rage which M. Perreard subsequently poured into my ear....

3.

When the Queen had explored all the woods and ravines close at hand, she naturally wished to extend the radius of her excursions. She was a fearless walker and was not to be thwarted by the steepest paths, even when these were filled with snow in which one's feet sank up to the ankles. I urgently begged the young sovereign never to venture far afield without first informing me of her intentions. As a matter of fact, I knew how easy it was to lose one's self in the maze of mountains, where one loses the trace of any road; and I was also afraid of unpleasant meetings, for Savoy is often infested with strangers from beyond the Piedmontese frontier who come to France in search of work.

Lastly there was "the black man." The legend of this black man was current throughout the district, where it spread a secret terror. Stories were told in the hamlet of a man dressed in black from head to foot, who roamed at nightfall through the neighbouring forests. He had eyes of fire and was frightfully lean.

The peasants were convinced that it was a ghost, for he never answered when spoken to and disappeared as soon as anyone drew near. I did not, of course, share the superstitious terrors of the inhabitants of the Corbières; but I thought that the ghost might be just some tramp or marauder and I did not care for the Queens to come across him. Imagine my alarm, therefore, when, one afternoon, after I had gone down to Aix-les-Bains, I was handed the following laconic telegram:

"Queen gone walk without giving notice late in returning."

To jump into the funicular railway and go back to the Corbières was for me the work of a few minutes. There I heard that Queen Wilhelmina had gone out with her two ladies-in-waiting, saying that she meant to take a little exercise, as she had not been out all day, and that she would be back in an hour. Two hours had since elapsed, the Queen had not returned and Queen Emma was beginning to feel seriously alarmed.

I at once rushed out in search of Her Majesty, questioning the people whom I met on my way. No one had seen her. I ran into the forest, where I knew that she was fond of going; I called out; no reply. More and more anxious, I was about to hunt in another direction, when my eyes fell upon traces of feet that had left their imprint on the snow. I examined them: the foot-prints were too small to belong to a man; they had evidently been made by women's shoes. I therefore followed the trail as carefully as an Indian hunter. Nor was I mistaken: after half-an-hour's walk, I heard clear voices calling out and soon I saw the little Queen arrive, happy and careless, followed by her two companions:

"Well, M. Paoli, you were running after us, I will bet. Just think, we got lost, without knowing, and were looking for our way. It was great fun!"

I did not venture to admit that I was far from sharing this opinion and I confined myself to warning the Queen that her mother was anxious.

"Then let us hurry back as fast as we can," she said, her face suddenly becoming overcast.

And I have no doubt that Her Majesty, on returning, was soundly scolded.

Strangely enough, I was able to lay my hand on "the black man" on the evening of the very same day. It was a very clear night, with the moon shining on the snow-clad mountains, and I resolved to go down to Aix on foot, instead of using the funicular railway. I therefore took the path that led through the wood; and, on reaching a glade at a few yards from the royal villa, I perceived a shadow that appeared to be hiding behind the trees.

"There's the famous black man," I thought.

But, as the shadow had all the air of an animal of the human species, I also contemplated the possible presence of an anarchist charged to watch the approaches to the royal residence. I took out my revolver and shouted:

"Who goes there?"

"I, monsieur le commissaire!" replied a familiar voice, while the shadow took shape, emerged from the trees, stepped forward and gave the military salute.

I then recognised one of my own inspectors, whom I had instructed to go the rounds of the precincts of the Queens' chalet nightly. He was the individual who had been taken for "the black man." However, he seemed none the worse for it.

4.

When the Queen had visited all the places in the immediate neighbourhood of the Corbières and tasted sufficiently of the pleasure of looking upon herself as a new Little Red Riding-hood in her wild solitudes, or a new Sleeping Beauty (whose Prince Charming was not to come until many years later), she expressed the wish to go on the longer excursions which the country-side afforded. We therefore set out, one fine morning, for the Abbey of Hautecombe, situated on the banks of the poetic Lac du Bourget, which inspired Lamartine with one of his most beautiful meditations.

Although standing on French territory, the old Abbey occupied by the Cistercian monks continues to belong to Italy, or, at least, remains the property of the royal house by virtue of an agreement made between the two governments at the time of the French annexation of Savoy in 1860. It contains forty-three tombs of Princes and Princesses of the House of Savoy. All the ancestors of King Victor-Emanuel, from Amadeus V to Humbert III lie under the charge of the White Fathers in this ancient monastery full of silence and majesty. Their mausoleums are carved, for the most part, by the chisels of illustrious sculptors; they stand side by side in the great nave of the chapel, which is in the form of a Latin cross, with vaults painted sky-blue and transepts peopled with upwards of three-hundred statues in Carrara marble. These, crowded together within that narrow fabric, form as it were a motionless and reflective crowd watching over the dead.

The visitor bends over the tombs and reads the names inscribed upon them; and all the adventurous, chivalrous, heroic and gallant history of the House of Savoy comes to life again. Here lies Amadeus, surnamed the Red Count, and Philibert I the Hunter; further on, we come to Maria Christina of Bourbon-Savoy, Joan of Montfort, and Boniface of Savoy, the prince who became Archbishop of Canterbury;[6] further still is the tomb of the young and charming Yolande of Montferrat, who sleeps beside her father, Aymon the Peaceful. Lastly, at the entrance of the church, in the chapel of Our Lady of the Angels, stands the sarcophagus of Charles Félix, King of Sardinia, who restored Hautecombe in 1842. The old standard of the Bodyguards of the Savoy Company shelters him beneath its folds, which have ceased to flutter many a long century ago.

This fine historical lesson within a monastic sanctuary interested the two Dutch Queens greatly. It made Queen Wilhelmina very thoughtful, especially at a given moment when the monk who acted as her guide said, with a touch of pride in his voice:

"The House of Savoy is a glorious house!"

After a second's pause, the little Queen replied:

"So is the House of Orange!..."

A few days after our excursion to Hautecombe, we went to visit the Cascade de Grésy, a sort of furious torrent in which Marshal Ney's sister, the Baronne de Broc, was drowned in 1818 before the eyes of Queen Hortense, the mother of Napoleon III. We also drove to the Gorges du Fier, in which no human being had dared to venture before 1869. Queen Wilhelmina, ever eager for emotional impressions, insisted on penetrating at all costs through the narrow passage that leads into the gorges. The Queen Mother lived through minutes of agony that day, although I did my best to persuade Her Majesty that her daughter was not really incurring any danger. But there is no convincing an anxious mother!

Stimulated by these various excursions, the little Queen said to me, one morning:

"M. Paoli, I have formed a great plan. My mother approves. I want to go and see the Grande Chartreuse."

"That is easily done," I replied, "but it will take a whole day, for the monastery is a good distance from here."

"Well, M. Paoli, arrange the excursion as you think best: with the snow on the ground, it will be magnificent!"

I wrote to the Father Superior to tell him of the Queen's wish. He answered by return that, to his great regret, he was unable to open the doors of the monastery to women, even though they were Queens, without the express authorisation of the Pope. And indeed I remembered that the same objection had arisen some years earlier, when I wanted to take Queen Victoria to the Grande Chartreuse: I had to apply to Rome on that occasion also.

I therefore hastened to communicate the answer to General Du Monceau, who at once telegraphed to Cardinal Rampolla, at that time Secretary of State to the Holy See. Cardinal Rampolla telegraphed the same evening that the Pope granted the necessary authority.

These diplomatic preliminaries gave an additional zest to our expedition. For it was a genuine expedition. We left Aix-les-Bains at eight o'clock in the morning, by special train, for Saint-Béron, which was then the terminus of the railway, before entering the great mountain. Here, two landaus with horses and postilions awaited us. The two Queens and their ladies stepped into one of the carriages; General Du Monceau, the officers of the suite and I occupied the other; and we started. It was eleven o'clock in the morning and we had a three hours' drive before us. Notwithstanding the intense cold, a flood of sunshine fell upon the immense frozen and deserted mountain-mass and lit up with a blinding flame the long sheets of snow that lay stretching to the horizon, where they seemed to be merged in the deep blue of the sky. No sign of life appeared in that sea of mountains, amid the throng of dissimilar summits, some blunt, some pointed, but all girt at their base with huge pine-forests. Only the rhythmical tinkling of our harness-bells disturbed the deep silence.

We began to feel the pangs of hunger after an hour's driving. I had foreseen that we should find no inn on the road and had taken care to have baskets of provisions stored in the boot of each carriage at Saint-Béron.

"That's a capital idea," said Queen Wilhelmina. "You shall lunch with us. I will lay the cloth!"

The carriages had stopped in the middle of the road, in the vast solitude, opposite the prodigious panorama of white mountains and gloomy valleys. The little Queen spread a large table-napkin over our knees. From the depths of a hamper, she produced a cold chicken, rolls and butter and solemnly announced:

"Luncheon is served."

Served by a Queen, in a carriage, on a mountain-top: that was an incident lacking to my collection, as King Alfonso would have said! I need hardly add that this picturesque luncheon was extremely lively and that not a vestige of it remained when, at two o'clock, we approached the Grande Chartreuse.

We caught sight first of the square tower, then of the great slate roofs, then of the countless steeples, until, at last, in the fold of a valley, the impressive block of buildings came into view, all grey amidst its white setting and backed by the snow-covered forests scrambling to the summit of the Col de la Ruchère. Perched amidst this immaculate steppe, among those spurs bristling with contorted and threatening rocks, as though in some apocalyptic landscape, the cold, stern, proud convent froze us with a nameless terror: it seemed to us as though we had reached the mysterious regions of a Wagnerian Walhalla; the fairy-tale had turned into a legend, through which the flaxen-haired figure of the little Queen passed like a light and airy shadow.

All the inhabitants of the monastery stood awaiting the Queens at the threshold of the gateway. The monks were grouped around their superior; their white frocks mingled with the depths of the immense corridor, the endless straight line of which showed through the open door.

The Father Superior stepped forward to greet the two Queens. Tall in stature, with the face of an ascetic, a pair of piercing eyes, an harmonious voice and a cold dignity combined with an exquisite courtesy, lie had the grand manner of the well-bred man of the world:

"Welcome to Your Majesties," he said, slowly, with a bow.

The Queens, a little awestruck, made excuses for their curiosity; and the inspection began. The monks led their royal visitors successively through the cloister, the refectories, the fine library, which at that time contained over twenty-thousand volumes, the rooms devoted to work and meditation, each of which bore the name of a country or province, because formerly they served as meeting-places for the priors of the charter-houses of each of those countries or provinces. They showed their kitchen, with its table formed of a block of marble nine yards long and its chimney of colossal proportions. They threw open the great chapter-house decorated with twenty-two portraits of the generals of the order from its foundation and furnished with lofty stalls in which the monks used to come and sit when, twice a year, they held their secret assembly. They showed their exiguous cells, with their tiled floors and whitewashed walls, each containing a truckle-bed, a praying-chair, a table, a crucifix and a window opening upon the vast and splendid horizon of the fierce mountains beyond. Lastly, they showed their church, with its Gothic carvings surmounted by a statue of death, and their desolate and monotonous cemetery, in which only the graves of the priors are distinguished by a wooden cross. But they did not show their relics and their precious sacred books. I expressed my astonishment at this; and one of the fathers replied, coldly:

"That is because the Queens are heretics. We only show them to Catholics."

Queen Wilhelmina, who had gradually recovered her assurance, plied the superior with questions, to which he replied with a perfect good grace. When, at last, the walk through the maze of passages and cloisters was finished, the Queen hesitated and then asked:

"And the chartreuse? Don't you make that here?"

"Certainly, Ma'am," said the prior, "but we did not think that our distillery could interest Your Majesty."

"Oh, but it does!" answered the Queen, with a smile. "I want to see everything."

We were then taken to the "Mill," situated at an hour's distance from the monastery, where the Carthusians, with their sleeves turned back, prepared the delicious liqueur the secret of which they have now taken with them in their exile. The Queens put their lips to a glass of yellow elixir offered to them by the superior and accepted a few bottles as a present. The visit had interested them prodigiously.

Half an hour later, we had left the convent far behind us in its stately solitude and were driving down the other slope of the mountain to Grenoble, where we were to find a special train to take us back to Aix-les-Bains. When we approached the old Dauphiné capital, the day had turned into a night of black and icy darkness; in front of us, in the depths of the valley, all the lamps of the great city displayed their thousands of twinkling lights; and Queen Wilhelmina kept on exclaiming:

"How beautiful! How delighted I am!"

She was not so well pleased—nor was I—when, at the gate of the town, we saw cyclists who appeared to be on the lookout for our carriages and who darted off as scouts before our landaus as soon as they perceived us. These mysterious proceedings were all the more insoluble to me as I had taken care not to inform the authorities of Grenoble that the Queens intended to pass through their city, knowing as I did, on the one hand, that the municipal council was composed of socialists and, on the other, that Their Majesties wished to preserve the strictest incognito. But I had reckoned without the involuntary indiscretion of the railway staff, who had allowed the fact to leak out that a special train had been ordered for the sovereigns; and, as no one is more anxious to receive a smile from royalty than the stern, uncompromising adherents of Messrs. Jaurès & Co., the first arm that was respectfully put out to assist Queen Wilhelmina to alight from the carriage was that of the socialist senator who, that year, was serving as Mayor of Grenoble. He was all honey; he had prepared a speech; he had provided a band. Willy-nilly, we had to submit to an official reception. True, we were amply compensated, as the train steamed out of the station, by hearing cries of "Long live the Queen!" issuing from the throats of men who spent the rest of the year in shouting, "Down with tyrants!"

Such is the eternal comedy of politics and mankind.

5.

The Queens' stay at the Corbières was drawing to a close. We had exhausted all the walks and excursions; the cold was becoming daily more intense; the icy wind whistled louder than ever under the ill-fitting doors. At the royal chalet, the little Queen was growing tired of sketching young herds with their flocks or old peasant-women combing wool. One morning, General Du Monceau said to me:

"Their Majesties have decided to go to Italy They will start for Milan the day after to-morrow."

Two days later, I left them at the frontier; and, as I was taking my leave of them:

"We shall meet again," said Queen Wilhelmina. "I am longing to see Paris."

She did not realise her wish until two years later. It was in the spring of 1898—a year made memorable in her life because it marked her political majority and the commencement of her real reign—that, accompanied by her mother, she paid a first visit to Paris on her way to Cannes for the wedding of Prince Christian cf Denmark (the present Crown-prince) and the Grand-duchess Mary of Mecklenburg-Strelitz.

"Do you remember the day when we went to the Grande Chartreuse?" were her first words on seeing me.

She still had her bright, childish glance, but she now wore her pretty hair done up high, as befitted her age, and her figure had filled out in a way that seemed to accentuate her radiant air of youth.

Anecdotes were told of her playfulness that contrasted strangely with her sedate appearance. Chief among them was the well-known story according to which she loved to tease her English governess, Miss Saxton Winter: all Holland had heard how, one day, when drawing a map of Europe, she amused herself by enlarging the frontiers of the Netherlands out of all proportion and considerably reducing those of great Britain. Another story was that, having regretfully failed to induce the postal authorities to alter her portrait on the Dutch stamps, which still represented her as a little girl, with her hair down, she never omitted with her own pen to correct the postage-stamps which she used for her private correspondence!

These childish ways did not prevent her from manifesting a keen interest in poetry and art. Her favourite reading was represented by Sir Walter Scott and Alexandre Dumas the Elder; but she also read books on history and painting with the greatest pleasure. She had acquired a remarkable erudition on these subjects in the course of her studies, as I had occasion to learn during our visits to the museums, especially the Louvre. She was familiar with the Italian and French schools of painting as with the Dutch and Flemish, although she maintained a preference for Rembrandt:

"I should like him to have a statue in every town in Holland!" she used to say.

Nevertheless, the artistic beauties of Paris did not, of course, absorb her attention to the extent of causing her to disregard the attractions and temptations which our capital offers to the curiosity of a young and elegant woman who does not scorn the fascination of dress. Queen Wilhelmina used to go into ecstasies over the beauty and luxury of our shops; and Queen Emma would have the greatest difficulty in dragging her from the windows of the tradesmen in the Rue Royale and the Rue de la Paix. It nearly always ended with a visit to the shop and the making of numerous purchases.

The little Queen won the affection of all with whom she came into contact by her simplicity, her frankness and the charming innocence with which she indulged in the sheer delight of living. Although possessed of an easy and ready admiration, she remained Dutch at heart and professed a proud and exclusive patriotism.

"I can understand," said President Félix Faure to me, on the day after the visit which he paid to the two Queens, "that the Dutch nation shows an exemplary loyalty to Queen Wilhelmina. It recognises itself in her."

Indeed, nowhere is the sovereign more securely installed than in Holland, nor does the work of government proceed anywhere more smoothly. In Holland, constitutional rule performs its functions automatically, while the budget balances regularly, year by year, thanks to the colonies and trade. Happy country. What other state can say as much to-day?

A week after their arrival in Paris, the two Queens left for Cannes. I had been called south by my service in waiting on Queen Victoria, who had just gone to Cannes herself, and I was obliged to leave a few days before Their Majesties. But I met them again at the Danish wedding, which was so picturesque and poetic in its Mediterranean setting.

I saw Queen Wilhelmina for the last time shortly before her departure for Holland. It was in the late afternoon, at the moment when the sun was on the point of disappearing behind the palm-trees in the garden of the hotel where the Queen of England had taken up her residence. Queen Wilhelmina had come to say good-bye; she was standing in an attitude of timid deference before the old sovereign seated in her bath-chair. Both Queens were smiling and talking merrily. Then Wilhelmina, stooped, kissed Queen Victoria on the forehead and tripped away lightly in the golden rays of the setting sun.

She has not returned to France since then.

VIII

THE LATE KING OF THE BELGIANS

1.

Of all the sovereigns with whom I have been connected in the course of my career, Leopold II is perhaps the one whom I knew best, with the circumstances of whose private life I was most intimately acquainted and whose thoughts and soul I was nevertheless least able to fathom, for the simple reason that his thoughts were impenetrable and his soul remained closed. Was this due to excessive egotism or supreme indifference? To both, perhaps. He was as baffling as a puzzle, carried banter occasionally to the verge of insolence and cynicism to that of cruelty; and, if, at times, he yielded to fits of noisy gaiety, if, from behind the rough exterior, there sometimes shot an impulse of unexpected kindness, these were but passing gleams. He promptly recovered his wonderful self-control; and those about him were too greatly fascinated by his intelligence to seek to understand his habit of mind or heart. And yet, though fascinating, he was as uncommunicative as it is possible to be; he possessed none of the external attractions of the intellect which captivate and charm; but, whenever he deigned to grant you the honour of an interview, however brief, you at once discovered in him a prodigious brain, a luminous perspicacity and critical powers of amazing subtlety and keenness.

No sovereign used—and abused—all the springs of his physical and moral activity, to a greater extent than did Leopold II to his dying day. An everlasting traveller, passing without cessation from a motor-car into a train, from a train on to a boat, caring little for the delights of sleep, he worked continuously, whether in the presence of some fine view, or at sea, or at meals, or in the train, or in his hotel, or on a walk; the place and the hour mattered to him but little.

"Monsieur l'officier, take down!" he would say to his equerry, at the most unexpected moment.

And "monsieur l'officier"—his only form of address for the officers of his suite—drew out a notebook, seized a pencil and took down "by way of memorandum," to the slow, precise and certain dictation of the king, the wording of a letter, a report or a scheme relating to the multifarious operations in which Leopold II was interested. Contrary to the majority of monarchs, who took with them on their holidays a regular arsenal of papers and a very library of records, Leopold carried in the way of reference books, nothing but a little English-French dictionary, which he slipped into the pocket of his overcoat and consulted for the purpose of the voluminous correspondence which he conducted in connexion with Congo affairs:

"It is no use my knowing English thoroughly," he confessed to me, one day. "Those British officials sometimes employ phrases of which I do not always grasp the full meaning and scope. I must fish out my lexicon!"

On the other hand, he had needed no assistance in order to work out his complicated and gigantic financial combinations. He possessed, if I may say so, the bump of figures. For hours at a time, he would indulge in intricate calculations and his accounts never showed a hesitation or an erasure. In the same way, when abroad, he treated affairs of state with a like lucidity. If he thought it useful to consult a specialist in certain matters, he would send for him to come to where he was, question him and send him away, often after teaching the expert a good many things about his own profession which he did not know before. And the king thereupon made up his mind in the full exercise of his independent and sovereign will.

"My ministers," he would say, with that jeering air of his, "are often idiots. But they can afford the luxury: they have only to do as I tell them."

Leopold II did not always, however, take this view of the constitutional monarchy. For instance, a few months before his death, one of his ministers was reading a report to him in the presence of the heir presumptive—now King Albert—when the wind, blowing through the open window of the royal waiting-room, sent a bundle of papers, on the King's desk, flying all over the carpet. The minister was rushing forward to pick them up, when the King caught him by the sleeve and, turning to his nephew, said:

"Pick them up yourself."

And, when the minister protested:

"Leave him alone," whispered Leopold. "A future constitutional sovereign must learn to stoop!"

An autocrat in his actions, he affected to be a democrat in his principles.

It matters little whether his methods were reprehensible or not: history will say that Leopold II was to Belgium the artisan of an unequalled prosperity, although it is true that he was nearly always absent from his country. The fact is that he loved France at least as well as Belgium. He loved the Riviera and, above all, he loved the capital. He had the greatest difficulty in dragging his white beard away from the Paris radius; and, when, by chance, it was eclipsed for a week or two, it continued to figure in the magazines, in the illustrated and comic papers and on the posters that advertised cheap tailors, tonic pills or recuperative nostrums. Leopold II, therefore, was a Parisian personality in the full glory of the word. True, he never achieved the air of elegance that distinguished Edward VII. You would have looked for him in vain on the balcony of the club, on the asphalt of the boulevards, in a stage-box at the theatre, in the paddock at Longchamp. But, should you happen to meet in the Tuileries Gardens, in the old streets of the Latin Quarter or, more likely still, along the quays, a man wrapped in a long dark ulster, wearing a pair of galoshes over his enormous boots and a black bowler on his head, carrying in his hand an umbrella that had seen better days and under his arm a bundle of yellow-backed books or a knickknack of some sort packed up anyhow in a newspaper; should you catch sight of a lean and lanky Ghent burgess rooted in silent contemplation of the front of the Louvre, or the porch of Saint-Germain-l'Auxerrois, or the gates of the École des Beaux-Arts; should you perceive him haggling for a musty old book at the corner of the Pont des Saints-Pères and counting the money twice over before paying, then you could safely have gone home and said:

"I saw the King of the Belgians to-day."

I often accompanied him on these strolls in the course of which the artist and book-lover that lay hidden in him found many an occasion for secret and silent joys; for the King, who hated music, who bored himself at the theatre and who despised every manifestation of the art of to-day, had a real passion for old pictures, fine architecture, rare curiosities and flowers.

"Monsieur le commissaire," he would often say, with his fondness for official titles, in his strong Belgian accent, "we will go for an excursion to-day with monsieur l'officier."

And the "excursion" nearly always ended by taking us to some old curiosity shop or to the Musée Carnavalet, or to the flower-market on the Quai de la Tournelle.

In the later years of his life, however, he had to give up his walks in town: he was attacked by sciatica, which stiffened his left leg and prevented him from walking except with the aid of two sticks or leaning on his secretary's arm. Also, the fact that he had—not always justly—been made the absurd hero of certain gay adventures, subjected him to an irksome popularity which caused him genuine annoyance. He was ridiculed in the music-halls and in the scandal-mongering press; caricatures of him were displayed in all the newsvendors' windows.

This stupid and sometimes spiteful interest in his movements was a positive affliction to him. We did our best, of course, to prevent his seeing the satirical drawings in which he figured in attitudes unbecoming to the dignity of a king; but we did not always succeed. Fortunately, his sense of humour exceeded any grudge which he may have felt. Remembering that he possessed an astonishing double in the person of an old Parisian called M. Mabille, he never failed to exclaim when, by some unlucky chance, his eyes fell upon a caricature of his royal features:

"There, they're teasing that unfortunate M. Mabille again! And how like me he is! Lord, how like me he is!"

His habit of icy chaff made one feel perpetually ill at ease when he happened to be in a conversational vein. One never knew if he was serious or joking. This tall, rough-hewn old man had a trick of stinging repartee under an outward appearance of innocent good-nature and, better than anyone that I have ever met, understood the delicate art of teaching a lesson to those who ventured upon an improper remark or an unseemly familiarity in his presence.

One evening, at a reception which he was giving to the authorities in his chalet at Ostende, the venerable rector of the parish came up to him with an air of concern and drawing him respectfully aside, said:

"Sir, I feel profoundly grieved. There is a rumour, I am sorry to say, that your Majesty's private life is not marked by the austerity suited to the lofty and difficult task which the Lord has laid upon the monarchs of this earth. Remember, Sir, that it behooves kings to set an example to their subjects."

And the worthy rector, taking courage from the fact that he had known Leopold II for thirty years, preached him a long sermon. The penitent, adopting an air of contrition, listened to the homily without moving a muscle. When, at last, the priest had exhausted his eloquence:

"What a funny thing, monsieur le curé!" murmured the King, fixing him with that cold glance of his, from under his wrinkled eyelids. "Do you know, people have told me exactly the same thing about you! Only I refused to believe it, you know!"[7]

That was a delicious sally, too, in which he indulged at the expense of a certain Brazilian minister, who was paying his first visit to court, and who appeared to be under the impression that the King was hard of hearing. At any rate, he made the most extraordinary efforts to speak loud and to pronounce his words distinctly. The King maintained an impassive countenance, but ended by interrupting him:

"Excuse me, monsieur le ministre," he said, with an exquisite smile. "I'm not deaf, you know: it's my brother!"

Picture the diplomatist's face!

Lastly, let me recall his caustic reply to one of our most uncompromising radical deputies, who was being received in audience and who, falling under the spell of King Leopold's obvious intelligence, said to him, point-blank:

"Sir, I am a republican. I do not hold with monarchies and kings. Nevertheless, I recognise your great superiority and I confess that you would make an admirable president of a republic!"

"Really?" replied the King, with his most ingenuous air. "Really? Do you know, I think I shall pay a compliment in your style to my physician, Dr. Thirier, who is coming to see me presently. I shall say, 'Thirier, you are a great doctor and I think you would make an excellent veterinary surgeon!'"

The poor opinion which he entertained of the republic, as this story would appear to show, did not prevent him from treating it with the greatest respect. Of all the foreign sovereigns, Leopold II was certainly the one who kept up the most cordial relations with our successive presidents. At each of his visits to Paris, he never failed to go to the Élysée. He called as a neighbour, as a friend without even announcing his visit beforehand. When M. Fallières was elected President at the Versailles congress, the first visit which he received, on his return to the Senate, where he was then living, was that of Leopold II.

Nevertheless, whatever personal sympathy he may have felt for France, the King of the Belgians always turned a deaf ear to sentimental considerations; and there is no reason why we should ascribe to such considerations the very marked courtesy which he showed to the official republican world. In my opinion, this attitude is due to several causes. In the first place, he reckoned that France was a useful factor in the development of Belgian prosperity and that it was wise to increase the economic links that united the two countries. On the other hand, what would have become of his colonial enterprise in the Congo, if France had taken sides with England, which was displaying a violent hostility against him? Lastly, this paradoxical monarch, who always governed through Catholic ministries at home, because that was the wish expressed by the majority of votes, was, I firmly believe, a free-thinker at heart and was pleased to find that our rulers entertained views which corresponded with his own secret tendencies.

The fact is that Leopold II looked at everything from two points of view: that of practical reality and that of his own selfishness. The King had in his veins the blood of the Coburgs mixed with that of the d'Orlèans, two highly intelligent families, but utterly devoid of sentiment or sensibility; and he treated life as an equation which it was his business to solve by any methods, no matter which, so long as the result corresponded with that which he had assigned to it beforehand.

He had an extraordinarily observant mind, was marvellously familiar with the character of his people, its weaknesses and its vanities and played upon these with the firm, yet delicate touch of a pianist who feels himself to be a perfect master of his instrument and of its effects. His cleverness as a constitutional sovereign consisted in appearing to follow the movements of public opinion, whereas, in reality, he directed and sometimes even provoked them.

Thus, in 1884, when the violent reaction of the Catholics against the anti-clerical policy of M. Frère-Orban culminated in the return of the conservatives to power, one might have thought that the Crown, which until then had supported the liberal policy and favoured the secularisation of the schools, would find itself in a curiously difficult position and that the check administered to M. Frère-Orban would amount to a check administered to the King himself. Not at all. Leopold II, sheltering himself behind his duties as a constitutional sovereign, became, from one day to the next, as firm a supporter of the Catholic party as he had been, till then, of the liberals. Nay, more, I have learnt since that he had a hand in the change of attitude on the part of parliament and the nation. As I have hinted above, his personal sympathies lay on the side of the liberal party; but, with the perspicacity that was all his own, he was not slow in perceiving the spectre of budding socialism which was beginning to loom behind Voltairean liberalism. He suspected its dangers; and he did not hesitate to give a sudden turn to the right to the ship of state of which he looked upon himself as the responsible pilot. And this position he maintained until the end of his days without, for a moment, laying aside any of his personal preferences.

2.

My first meeting with Leopold II dates back to 1896. The King had prone to the Riviera, accompanied by his charming daughter, Princess Clémentine, now Princess Napoleon, who, from that time onward, filled in relation to her father the part of the Antigone of a tempestuous old age. I shall never forget my surprise when the King, who had made the long railway-journey from Brussels to Nice without a stop, said to his chamberlain, Baron Snoy, as they left the station:

KING LEOPOLD II.

"Send away the carriage, monsieur le chambellan. We'll go to the hotel on foot. I want to stretch my legs a bit!"

We walked down the Avenue Thiers, followed by an inconvenient little crowd of inquisitive people. Just as we were about to cross a street, a landau drove up and obliged us to step back to the pavement. As it passed us, the King solemnly took off his hat: he had recognised Queen Victoria seated in the carriage and apparently astonished at this unexpected meeting.

When we reached the Place Masséna, again the King's hat flew off: this time, it was the Dowager Empress of Russia entering a shop.

"The place seems crammed with sovereigns," he said, with his mocking air. "Whom am I going to meet next, I wonder?"

I saw little of him during this first short stay which he made at Nice, for I was at that time attached to the person of the Queen of England and had to transfer the duty of protecting King Leopold to one of my colleagues. I used to meet him occasionally—always on foot—on the Cimiez road; I would also see him, in the afternoon, taking tea at Rumpelmayer's with his two daughters, the Princesses Clémentine and Louise, and his son-in-law, Prince Philip of Saxe-Coburg-Gotha. These family meetings around a five o'clock tea-table marked the last auspicious days of peace which was more apparent than real among those illustrious personages.

When Leopold II returned to the Riviera two years later, he had quarrelled, in the meanwhile, with his daughter Louise, who herself had quarrelled with her husband; he had ceased to see his daughter Stéphanie, who had married Count Lonyay; and he met his wife, Queen Marie Henriette, as seldom as he possibly could. Princess Clémentine was the only one who still found favour with this masterful old man, who was so hard upon others and so indulgent to himself; and she continued, with admirable devotion and self-abnegation, to surround him with solicitous care and to accompany him wherever he went.

I never met a more smiling resignation than that of this princess, who took a noble pride in the performance of her duty. Nothing was able to discourage her in the fulfilment of her filial mission: not the rebuffs and caprices which she encountered on her father's side, nor the frequently delicate and sometimes humiliating positions which he forced upon her, nor even the persistency with which, until his dying day, he thwarted the secret inclinations of her heart.

It has been said that, at one time, he thought of giving her the Prince of Naples—now King of Italy—for a husband and that he abandoned the idea in consequence of the stubborn opposition which the plan encountered on the part of exalted political personages. I do not know if he ever entertained this plan; on the other hand, I feel pretty sure that, some years ago, he would have liked the Count of Turin for a son-in-law and that negotiations were even opened to this effect with the Italian court. But the most invincible of arguments—the only one that had not been taken into account—was at once opposed to this project: the princess's affections were engaged elsewhere. She loved Prince Victor Napoleon and had resolved that she would never marry another man. Of course, I was not present at the scene which the plain expression of this wish provoked between father and daughter; but I understand that it was of a violent character. From that day, the Prince's name was never mentioned between them. The Princess continued, as in the past, to fill the part of an attentive and devoted daughter; she continued scrupulously to perform her duties as "the little Queen," as the Belgians called her after 1904, the year of her mother's death, when she began to take Marie Henriette's place at official functions; she continued to succour the poor and nurse the sick with greater solicitude than ever; and she was seen, as before, driving her pony-chaise in the Bois de la Cambre. Only, in the privacy of her boudoir, the moment she had a little time to herself, she would immerse herself in the study of historical memoirs of the Napoleonic period.

To tell the truth, I believe that if Prince Victor had not possessed the grave fault, in Leopold's eyes, of being a pretender to the French throne, the King would have ended by giving to the daughter whom he adored the consent for which she vainly entreated during six long years. But the King was an exceedingly selfish man; he was eager, for the reasons explained above, to preserve good relations with the French Republic; and he refused at any price to admit the heir of the Bonapartes into his family. The result was that he ended by conceiving against the Prince the violent antipathy which he felt for any person who stood in his way and interfered with his calculations. I remember realising this one morning at the station at Bâle, where I had gone to meet him. The King was waiting on the platform for the Brussels train, when I suddenly caught sight of Prince Victor leaving the refreshment-room. I thought it my duty to tell the King.

"Oh, indeed!" he said. "Let's go and look at the engines."

And he strode away.

Can it have been because he was sure of meeting neither Prince Victor nor the members of his family on the Riviera that he resolved, at the end of his life, to fix one of his chief residences in the south of France? I will not go so far as to say so. I am more inclined to believe that the old King, who was a passionate lover of sunshine, flowers and freedom, found in that charming and easy-going country the environment most in harmony with his moods and tastes.

As early as 1898, he resolved to lay out for himself a paradise in that wonderful property, known as Passable, which he had purchased near Nice, with its gardens sloping down to the Gulf of Villefranche. He devoted all his horticultural and architectural knowledge, all his sense of what was beautiful and picturesque to its embellishment. Tiberius achieved no greater success at Capri. Year after year, he enlarged it, for he had a mania for building and pulling down. He also had the soul of a speculator. None knew better than he how to bargain for a piece of land: he would bully, threaten and intimidate the other side until he invariably won the day. Thereupon he used to indulge in childish delight:

"It's all right," he would say, with a great chuckle. "I have done a capital stroke of business!"

And I am bound to admit that he spared neither time nor energy when he scented what he called a "capital stroke of business."

I can still see him, one afternoon, leaving M. Waldeck-Rousseau's villa at the Cap d'Antibes, near Cannes, where he had gone to pay the prime minister a visit, and perceiving, on the road leading to the station, a magnificent walled-in park that looked as if it were abandoned:

"Who owns that property?" he asked, suddenly.

"An Englishman, Sir, who never comes near it."

"We have time to look over it," said the King, "before the train leaves for Nice. Somebody fetch the gardener!"

The gardener was not to be found, but the gate was open. Leopold II walked in, without hesitation, followed by Baron Snoy, my colleague, M. Olivi, and myself, hurried along the deserted paths and praised the beauty of the vegetation; but, when it became time to go, we discovered, to our dismay, that someone had locked the gate while we were inside. There was no key, no possibility of opening it. We called and shouted in vain. Nobody appeared. The train was due before long; the King began to grow impatient. What were we to do? Olivi had a flash of genius. He ran to a shed, the roof of which shewed above the nearest thicket, and returned with a ladder:

"If Your Majesty does not mind, you will be able to get over the wall."

The King accepted impassively and the ascent began. Baron Snoy went first, then I; and the King, in his turn, climbed the rungs, supported by Olivi. Baron Snoy and I, propped up on the top of the wall, hoisted the King after us. We were joined by Olivi; and then a dreadful thing happened: the ladder swayed and fell! There we were, all four of us, astride the wall, swinging our legs, without any means of getting down on the other side.

"We look like burglars," said the King, with a forced laugh.

There was nothing for it but to jump. The distance from the top of the wall to the slope beside the road was not great; and Baron Snoy, Olivi and I succeeded in falling on our feet without great difficulty. The King, however, who limped in one leg and lacked agility, could not think of it.

Then Olivi, who certainly proved himself a most resourceful man that day, solved the problem. He suggested that the King should climb down upon our shoulders. The King, accordingly, let himself slide down on to the shoulders of Baron Snoy, who passed him on to Olivi's back, while I caught hold of his long legs and deposited his huge feet safely on the ground!

Some years later, seeing Olivi at the station at Nice:

"I remember you, M. Olivi," said Leopold II. "You took part in our great gymnastic display at Antibes."

"I did, Sir."

"Well, do you know, M. Olivi, there is no need for me to climb the wall now. I have the key: the property belongs to me!"

The whole man is pictured in this anecdote. Even as he gave numberless signs of avarice and meanness in the details of material life, so he displayed an almost alarming extravagance once it became a question of satisfying a whim, although he would carefully calculate the advantages of any such whim beforehand. Now to increase the number of his landed properties was with him a genuine monomania, a sort of methodical madness.

At the bottom of his character lay certain precepts which belonged to the great middle class of 1840 and which had survived from the middle-class education imparted to him in his youth. It was thus that he was brought to think that the amount of a man's wealth is to be measured by the amount of real estate which he possesses. He fought shy of stocks and shares because of the frequent fluctuations to which they are subjected. On the other hand, he felt a constant satisfaction—I was almost saying a rapturous delight—in the acquisition of land, in turning his cash into acres of soil and investing his fortune in marble or bricks and mortar, because he looked upon these as more solid and lasting.

It goes without saying that, during his long visits to the South, he escaped as much of the official and social drudgery as he could. He saw very little of his illustrious cousins staying on the Riviera; avoided dinners and garden-parties; and, when not at work, spent his time in long and interminable walks, or else went and sat on a bench in some public garden or by the sea and there steeped himself in his reflexions. Sometimes, when he was in a hurry to get back, he would take the tram or hail a fly, always picking out the oldest and shabbiest.

One day, at his wish, I beckoned to a driver on the rank at Nice.

"No, no, not that one," he said. "Call the other man, over there: the one with the horse that looks half-dead."

"But the carriage seems very dirty, Sir," I ventured to remark.

"Just so: as he drives such an uninviting conveyance, he must be doing bad business; we must try and help him."

Leopold II had a trick of performing these sudden and unexpected acts of kindness.

He was a sceptic to the verge of indifference and yet entertained odd antipathies and aversions. For instance, he hated the piano and was terrified of a cold in the head. Whenever he had to select a new aide-de-camp, he always began by asking two questions:

"Do you play the piano? Do you catch cold easily?"

If the officer replied in the negative, the King said, "That's all right," and the aide-de-camp was appointed; but if, by ill-luck, the poor fellow returned an evasive answer, his fate was doomed: he went straight back to his regiment.

This inexplicable dread of the *corizza* had attained such proportions that, during the last years of the King's life, the people about him—including the ladies—discovered a simple and ingenious expedient for obtaining a day's leave when they wanted it: they simply sneezed without stopping. At the third explosion, the old sovereign gave a suspicious look at the sneezer and said:

"I sha'n't want you to-day."

And the trick was done.

On the other hand, he showed himself very indulgent towards his younger officers' adventures in the world of gallantry. I remember his chaffing one of them, one morning, at Nice. Captain Binjé, an officer whose intelligence, activity and devotion had earned his appreciation, was a little late on duty that morning; and moreover his clothes emitted a very strong scent. The King at once began to sniff:

"Oof! Oof!" he said. "I'll wager you struck a flower on your road here!"

"Y-your M-majesty," stammered the officer.

"All right, all right, my boy: you can't help it, at your age!"

He had idiosyncrasies, like most mortals. For instance, he used to have four buckets of sea-water dashed over his body every morning, by way of a bath; he expected partridges to be served at his meals all the year round; and he had his newspapers ironed like pocket-handkerchiefs before reading them: he could not endure anything like a fold or crease in them. Lastly, when addressing the servants, he always spoke of himself in the third person. Thus he would say to his chauffeur, "Wait for *him*," instead of, "Wait for *me*." Those new to his service, who had not been warned, were puzzled to know what mysterious person he referred to.

A strange eccentric, you will say. No doubt, although these oddities are difficult to understand in the case of a man who displayed the most practical mind, the most lucid intelligence and the shrewdest head for business the moment he was brought face to face with the facts of daily life. But, I repeat, to those who knew him best, he appeared in the light of a constant and bewildering puzzle; and this was shown not only in the peculiarity of his manners, but in the incongruity of his sentiments. How are we to explain why this King should feel an infinite love for children, this stern King who was so hard and sometimes so cruel in his treatment of those to whom by rights he ought never to have closed his heart nor refused his indulgence? Yet the tall old man worshipped the little tots. They were almost the only creatures whose greetings he returned; and he would go carefully out of his way, when strolling along a beach, rather than spoil their sand-castles. How are we to explain the deep-seated, intense and jealous delight which he, so insensible to the softer emotions of mankind, felt at the sight of the fragile beauty of a rare flower? How are we to explain why he reserved the kindness and gentleness which he so harshly refused to his wife and daughters for his unfortunate sister, the Empress Charlotte, whose mysterious madness had kept her for forty-two years a lonely prisoner within the high walls of the Château de Bouchout? And yet, every morning of those forty-two years he never failed, when at Laeken, to go alone across the park to that silent dwelling and spend two hours in solitary converse with the tragic widow. Each day, with motherly solicitude, he personally supervised the smallest details of that shattered existence.

Lastly, what an astounding contrast was offered in Leopold II, who was considered insensible to the weaknesses of the heart, by the sudden blossoming of a sentimental idyll in the evening of his life!

3.

No one, I said, at the beginning of this chapter, was more intimately acquainted than myself with the private life of the late King Leopold. This was one of the consequences—I am far from adding, one of the advantages—of my professional duties about the persons of the sovereigns whom I have guarded. And I would certainly have hesitated before broaching the subject of the royal adventures, if this subject had remained secret. But public animosity and the King's indifference to scandal have made it so well-known that I feel no scruples about speaking in my own turn, the more so as this will give me the opportunity of destroying many a detail of the legend which people have been pleased to build up around him and of correcting those facts which have come to the inquisitive ears of the public.

To begin with, the adventure with which Leopold II was credited for ten years in connexion with Mlle. Cléo de Mérode must be relegated to the pure domain of fiction. I daresay that it assisted the advancement of the young and pretty dancer as much as it annoyed the King, who was pursued even in Brussels itself by the irreverent nickname of "Cléopold." What gave rise to this absolutely gratuitous conviction on the part of public opinion? Nothing more nor less than a gossiping remark let fall in the slips at the Opera by someone who pretended that he had met the King and the ballet-dancer looking for a sequestered spot in the Forest of Saint-Germain.

The scandal was hardy and tough: it ran for ten years without stopping to take breath. At the end of that period, which was long enough to turn any lie into a truth, Leopold II, one night at the Opera, asked an important official to present Mlle. de Mérode to him, saying that he had never met the lady, although he had "often heard of her." The important official promptly adopted the view that the King was uncommonly "deep."

And yet it was perfectly true: he had never set eyes on her in his life. The fact was proved by the candour of the words which he addressed to the charming dancer when she was brought up to be presented:

"Allow me to express all my regrets if the good-fortune which people attribute to me has offended you at all. Alas, we no longer live in the days when a king's favour was not looked upon as compromising! Besides, I am only a little king."

On the other hand, a single and decisive love, which he preserved until his death was soon to fill his thoughts exclusively and graft upon his senile heart a belated bloom of disconcerting youth. When Leopold II made the acquaintance of Mlle. Blanche Caroline Delacroix, whom he afterwards raised to the dignity of Baroness Vaughan, he had just reached his sixty-fifth year. The lady boasted two-and-twenty summers. The humbleness of her birth prevented her from raising her eyes to a throne. She was the thirteenth child of a working mechanic and was born at Bucharest, where her father had gone to seek his fortune. She was brought up, therefore, in courts which were very different from royal courts; and I need not say that her education had hardly prepared her for the brilliant destiny which her chequered life held in store for her.

Well, one afternoon in September, she was sent for to be presented to King Leopold, who was passing through Paris, who had heard of her attractions and who felt interested in her modest condition. She was so flustered by this event that she promptly mixed up Belgium and Sweden. This was not a very serious matter in itself; but it might have been, in the circumstances, if Leopold II had not happened to be in a good humour that day. The fact remained that Mlle. Delacroix was convinced that she was in the presence of the King of Sweden, nor did she find out her mistake until she noticed the amused surprise which Leopold betrayed whenever, with her very comprehensible ignorance of the rules of etiquette, Mlle. Delacroix went out of her way to call him "His Majesty Oscar."

I am bound to confess that she at once recovered her self-possession when the King of the Belgians thought fit discreetly to apprise her of his identity and she was greatly diverted by her blunder. Two years later, I described the mishap to the King of Sweden, who happened to be staying at Biarritz at the same time as the Baroness Vaughan. Said Oscar II:

"Do present my fair cousin, who did me so great an honour!"

"But, Sir," I replied, "she may feel a regret!"

PRINCESS CLEMENTINE

"Do you think so, Paoli? And yet I am no 'fresher' than my cousin of Belgium. I am afraid, you see, that the regret will be all on my side!"

I believe that the regret was mutual. However, the meeting was arranged. The baroness took a snapshot of King Oscar with her kodak; and we agreed to say nothing about it to King Leopold, who was of a jealous disposition.

To what did Blanche Caroline Delacroix owe her success with Leopold II: to her vivid conversational powers, to the dazzling youthfulness of the fair-haired divinity that she was, or to her genuine intelligence? I cannot tell; but this much is certain, that, at her first audience, she succeeded in arousing in the old man's heart a love which was manifested at first in a polite flirtation and consecrated later in a union the mystery of which was never fully solved. Both the King and Mme. de Vaughan carefully refrained from making the smallest confidence on the subject of their marriage even to those in whom they confided most readily. Nevertheless, I have always believed that a secret religious ceremony did take place, so as to regularise their situation, if not with regard to Belgian law, at least in respect to the Church and their consciences. This conviction on my part was strengthened by the pastoral letter which Mgr. Mercier, Archbishop of Mechlin addressed to the Belgian Catholics after the King's death and in which the primate declared that the sovereign had died at peace with the Church of Rome. Allowing for the legitimate susceptibilities of the royal family, it was impossible to confirm the existence of a morganatic union in a more diplomatic manner. Some have said that the marriage was celebrated at San Remo, during the time when the King and Mme. de Vaughan were staying at Villefranche, near Nice. I cannot certify this. When I consult my recollection, I merely remember that, on a certain morning, some years before Leopold II's death, I saw the King and Mme. de Vaughan drive off together in a motor-car—a thing which they had never done before—he looking very nervous and she greatly excited. They forbade anyone to accompany them and did not return until evening, when they made no attempt to tell us where they had been. Marcel, the chauffeur, said that he had taken them to San Remo, on Italian territory; but, apart from this, he also showed a memorable discretion and we got no more out of him.

I noticed, however, that, from that day, the attitude of the couple changed: they showed themselves in public together, went openly to the theatre at Nice and to the carnival masquerade and abstained from taking the very childish and rather ridiculous precautions which the King had prescribed during the period of flirtation and "engagement" on the score of "saving appearances!"

Ridiculous and childish they were, as the reader can judge for himself. For instance, although the Baroness Vaughan shared all the King's journeys and accompanied him wherever he went, she was never to address a word to him in public or appear to know him. They took the same trains, got out at the same stations, put up at the same hotels in adjoining rooms, lunched and dined in the same dining-room, but ignored each other's existence, he with an imperturbable composure, she with a charming awkwardness.

The King never spoke of Mme. de Vaughan to the members of his suite: I do not believe that he once so much as mentioned her name before me; and yet *he knew that I knew*. He was quite aware that I had made her acquaintance and that we used to spend hours chatting together in the halls of the hotels at which we stayed. On the other hand, he imagined that nobody except myself suspected this intrigue, although it was an open secret about which the whole staff of the hotel, from the manager to the kitchen-scullions, used to gossip from morning till night! He went on stoically playing his puerile comedy. Every day, at lunch, seated with her maid at a table opposite him, she used to send smiles and signals to Captain Binjé and myself, who had our work cut out to keep a serious countenance. When lunch was over, Leopold would start on a walk with his aide-de-camp, while Mme. de Vaughan would set out, on her side, accompanied either by her companion or her maid. Half an hour later, they met on the high-road. The King would hurry forward, take off his hat and exclaim:

"Fancy meeting you, madame! How fortunate!"

This was the signal. The aide-de-camp and the lady's maid withdrew discreetly, leaving the two love-birds to themselves. They strolled together for a couple of hours, after which each took a different road back to the hotel, so as not to enter it at the same time.

On rainy days, the little scene was enacted with the aid of motor-cars. At a given spot, the King changed into Mme. de Vaughan's car, while the maid stepped into the King's. When, as sometimes happened, the baroness grew weary of this sentimental progress—for she had her capricious moods—she hastened to resort to the traditional method which never failed to achieve its object: she gave a sneeze, a loud, Titanic sneeze. Thereupon Leopold II forgot his tender passion and eagerly urged her to go home at once.

The Baroness Vaughan was not a bad sort of woman on the whole. In the early days, she used to put up with the violent outbursts to which the King occasionally treated her: she would light a great, big cigar and think no more about it. Afterwards, when she grew accustomed to look upon herself as the King's morganatic wife, her ambition increased and she insisted on being treated with deference. She complained to me that the Princess Clémentine, whom she had met on the road or in some path in a garden, had not condescended to return her bow; and she added, in a regretful tone:

"To think that, if I had lived in the days of Louis XIV, I should have had a stool at Court!"

In the absence of a stool, she managed to achieve a most luxurious existence. The King, who now never left her, had installed her, when he was in residence in Brussels, in a charming villa which communicated directly with the grounds of the Château de Laeken by means of a bridge that spanned the road and led into the Baroness Vaughan's garden. Every day, before paying her his visit, he sent her the choicest flowers from his hot-houses and the finest fruit in his orchard.

He also gave her a delightful little house on his estate of Passable, near Nice. He used to go there in the evening alone, through the garden, armed with a dark lantern, and spend two hours with the baroness playing cards. At eleven o'clock, he went back to his own villa, again carrying his dark lantern, while my detectives, crouching in the bushes, watched over his safety without his seeing them, although he knew that they were there; for, without showing it, he attached great importance to being properly guarded.

He was very thrifty in his personal expenditure and ended by imparting his habits of economy to his fair friend. Baroness Vaughan used to scrutinise the kitchen accounts as closely as any middle-class housewife. True, the housekeeping books sometimes took excessive liberties. I remember, one year at the Château de Lormois near Fontainebleau, which the King had hired for the season from Mme. Constant Say, the widow of the sugar-refiner, there was a violent scene with the cook, who had had the temerity to charge for seventy-five eggs in six days. Mme. de Vaughan was justly annoyed, dismissed him on the spot and refused to pay him the usual wages instead of notice. But Master Cook declined to be done out of what he considered his rights. In his fury, he hit upon the bright idea of taking up his stand, day after day, outside the gate of the château, where he launched out into invectives against his late mistress and loudly bewailed the injustice with which he pretended to have been treated. We dared not arrest him because of the scandal which he threatened to raise: he knew the habits of the house, of course. My detectives tried in vain to make him listen to reason and we were beginning to despair, when, at the end of a week, we saw that he was wearying of his daily pilgrimage. One fine day, he left for Paris and was seen no more.

Great as was the influence which Mme. de Vaughan had gained over the King's mind, I am bound to confess that it was never exercised in political matters nor in any of Leopold's financial undertakings. The baroness knew nothing about those things and made no attempt to understand them. The King was grateful to her for this discretion, which in reality was only indifference, for he never allowed any outsider to interfere in his affairs, whether public or private. He discussed none of his schemes before they were completed or before he had drawn up his plan of execution down to the minutest details.

"It shall be so," he used to declare; and no one ever dreamt of opposing his will so plainly expressed.

It was in this way that he conducted his enormous Congo enterprise entirely by himself. The different phases of this business are too well known for me to recapitulate them here. One of them, however—the first phase—has been very seldom discussed and deserves to be recalled, for it throws a great light not only upon the king's conceptive genius, but also upon his diplomatic astuteness and his amazing cynicism.

In 1884, Leopold II, who had for years been obsessed by the longing to lay hands upon the Congo territory, promoted an international conference in order to frustrate the West African treaty which had lately been concluded between Great Britain and Portugal and which stood in the way of the realisation of his secret ambitions. The King of the Belgians now conceived the subtle and intelligent idea of inducing the congress to proclaim the Congo into an independent state, with himself as its recognised sovereign.

There was only one person in Europe possessed of sufficient authority to bring about the adoption of this daring plan; and that was Bismarck. Bismarck was the necessary instrument; but how was he to be persuaded? Faced with this difficulty, Leopold II hit upon the idea of sending to Berlin a mere journalist, whom he knew to be a clever and talented man, and instructed him to capture the Iron Chancellor's confidence. Leopold coached this journalist, a gentleman of the name of Gantier, to such good purpose that, as the result of a campaign directed from Brussels by the King himself, M. Gantier managed, within a few months, to insinuate himself into Bismarck's immediate surroundings, to interest him in the Congo question and to prove to him that Germany would derive incomparable benefits from proclaiming the independence of the Congo and entrusting its administration to a neutral sovereign like the King of the Belgians.

The stratagem was successful from start to finish. The Congress of Berlin, on the motion of the chancellor, proclaimed the Congo an independent territory with Leopold II, for its sovereign. We know the result: the Congo is at this day a Belgian colony. Leopold II, in a word, had "dished" Prince Bismarck.

This incident is enough to show why the King considered himself superior to all his advisers and why, as I have already said, he felt grateful to Mme. de Vaughan for never talking to him about his vast enterprises. Her reticence made him appreciate her society all the more.

The relaxation which he found became more and more necessary to him because as he drew nearer the tomb, the worries aforesaid and his activities increased. It was as though he had received a mysterious warning to tell him that his years were now numbered and that he must hasten the realisation of his numerous and immense schemes. Not to speak of his work on the Congo, which was violently attacked both by politicians of all parties abroad and by the Opposition at home, his other vast undertakings also became the object of fierce criticism on the part of his adversaries, who considered that he was neglecting the political evolution of the country in order to devote himself entirely to his plans for transforming the town of Brussels. He was so well aware of this state of opinion that, when the burgomaster of the capital, his friend and fellow worker, M. Mott, came to congratulate the King on his last birthday, Leopold said:

"Let us hope that I shall have time to complete my work."

"Why not, Sir?" replied M. Mott. "You and I are of the same age; and You are stronger and haler than I am."

"Never mind, Monsieur le Bourgmestre: remember that, when one of us closes his eyes, the other will have to keep his open!"

It was written, in fact, that Leopold II should be called away before fully realising his colossal dreams and settling his intricate personal affairs. He was working up to the very moment of his death; as everybody knows, his mind remained clear to the end, nor did his hostility towards his family waver for an instant. He died as he had lived, inaccessible, haughty and sceptical.

Nay, even after he had entered into everlasting rest, he made one last effort to resist the final annihilation. I have the gruesome story from one of Leopold's aides-de-camp. On the night after the King's death, while two Sisters of Charity and an officer with drawn sword were watching by the remains in the *chapelle ardente*, suddenly an uncanny cracking sound was heard to issue from the coffin. The watchers at first believed it an hallucination; then, when the cracking continued and became louder and louder, the two nuns examined the bier. How great was their terror when, through the crevices in the wood, they saw the buttons of the uniform in which the King was clad and the hilt of his sword moving slowly upwards! The doctors were hurriedly sent for and declared that the deleterious gases were escaping from the ill-embalmed body, causing the King's corpse to swell and burst its coffin.

Thus death itself, after depriving him of movement for all time, refused him the majesty and mystery wherewith it surrounds all those whom it strikes, until the moment when they are lowered into the tomb!

IX

THE ENGLISH ROYAL FAMILY

1.

While writing these recollections, I have more than once had occasion, in passing, to mention different "faces" belonging to the Royal Family of England. They occur at most of the sovereign courts; for it was no empty phrase that used to describe Queen Victoria as "the grandmother of Europe." There was never a truer saying. Even as, in whichever direction beyond-seas we turn our eyes, we behold the British flag waving in the breeze, in the same way, if we study the pedigree of any royal house, we are almost always certain to discover an English alliance.

The long years which I spent in the service of Queen Victoria and the confidence with which she honoured me by admitting me to her intimacy enabled me to become acquainted with several members of that large, united and affable family; and I am bound to say that not one of them has forgotten me. They all deign to give me a little corner in their childish and youthful memories; they are good enough to remember that, in the old days, when they came to Nice, to Aix, to Biarritz or to Cannes to pay their duty to their grandmother and to bring her the smile of their youth, there was always in the old-fashioned landau that carried the good Queen along the country roads, or walking beside her donkey-chair, somebody who shared the general gaiety and whom the Queen treated with affectionate kindness. That "somebody" was myself.

I thus had the honour of seeing King George V when he was still wearing the modest uniform of a lieutenant in the Royal Navy and, later, of knowing Queen Mary when she was only Duchess of York and Cornwall. And I hope that she will permit me, in this connexion, to recall an incident that diverted Queen Victoria's little circle for a whole evening. It happened during a visit which the Duchess of York was paying to the Queen at Nice. I had informed the venerable sovereign that the "ladies of the fishmarket"—one of the oldest corporations at Nice—wished to offer her some flowers; and the Queen asked the Duchess of York to receive them in her stead and to express her sincere thanks for their good wishes.

The good women handed the Duchess their bouquets; and I then saw that they were shy and at a loss what to do or say next. So I whispered to them:

KING EDWARD VII

"Go and kiss that gentleman over there," pointing to Colonel Carington, the Queen's equerry. "That is by far the best speech that you could make!"

The ladies evidently approved of my suggestion, for they forthwith, one and all, flung themselves upon the colonel's neck; and he, though flurried and a little annoyed, had to submit with the best grace possible to this volley of kisses under the eyes of the princess, who laughed till the tears ran down her cheeks.

When I apologised to him afterwards for the abominable trick which I had played him:

"Ah," he sighed, "if only they had been good-looking!"

The fact is that none of the ladies evoked the most distant memories of the Venus of Milo!

Thanks to the recollections of those bygone years, of which any number of charming and amusing stories could be told, I was no longer a stranger to the Duke and Duchess of York when, after the accession of King Edward VII, they were raised to the title of Prince and Princess of Wales and travelled across France, under my protection, on their way to Brindisi, where they were to take ship for India.

"I will present you to the prince myself," said Princess May, with exquisite and simple kindliness, when she saw me waiting for them in the railway station at Calais. And she continued, "George, this is M. Paoli: you remember him, don't you?"

"I remember," said the prince, giving me his hand, "how much my grandmother liked you and the affection which she showed you. I need hardly say that we feel just the same to you ourselves."

I could not have hoped for a more cordial welcome from the prince, whose features bore so striking a resemblance to those of the Emperor of Russia, whom I had just left.

This journey was a particularly pleasant one for me, as it enabled me to foregather once more with an old and faithful friend in the person of the prince's secretary, of whom I had seen a great deal at the time when he was private secretary to Queen Victoria and who now occupies the same position under King George V; I refer to Sir Arthur Bigge.

Sir Arthur belongs to that race of servants of the monarchy whose zeal and devotion cease only with their death. He met with a striking adventure at the time of the interview between Queen Victoria and the late M. Félix Faure at Noisy-le-Sec. The story has never been told before; and I have no hesitation in publishing it, because it does great credit to the generosity of feeling of the then President of the Republic.

The Queen was on her way to Nice, that year, and had expressed a wish to meet M. Félix Faure, whom she did not know. The interview was arranged to take place during the stop of the royal train at Noisy Junction; and it had acquired a certain solemnity owing to the political circumstances of the moment. We began by witnessing a long private conversation between the Queen and the president through the windows of the royal saloon-carriage, after which, in accordance with the usual etiquette, they presented the members of their respective suites. When it came to Colonel Bigge's turn, the Queen said to M. Faure, without having the least idea of mischief in her mind:

"My private secretary, Sir Arthur Bigge, who enjoys all my confidence and all my esteem. Besides, I expect you know his name: it was he who accompanied the Empress Eugénie on her sad pilgrimage to Zululand and helped her to recover the body of her poor son."

The president bowed, without moving a muscle of his face or uttering a word; and Sir Arthur, greatly embarrassed by the terms of the presentation, thought the best thing for him to do was to lie low and keep out of the way.

How great, therefore, was his surprise when, after everybody had been presented, he heard his name called by M. Félix Faure:

"What can he want with me?" he asked, rather uneasily.

As soon as they were alone, the president said to him, point-blank:

"As a Frenchman, I wish to thank you for the devotion which you have shown to one of our fellow-countrywomen in circumstances so terrible for her. You behaved like a man of heart. I congratulate you."

M. Faure had the knack of enhancing the character of his office and winning the respectful sympathy of foreigners by happy flashes of inspiration of this kind.

But I am wandering from my subject. To return to the Prince of Wales, the cordiality of the reception which he gave me at Calais promised me a charming journey. In point of fact, I was able, during the run across France, to perceive how fond both the prince and princess were of simplicity and gaiety. They were evidently delighted to be going to India, although the princess could not accustom herself to the idea of leaving her children. As for the prince, he was revelling beforehand in the length of the voyage:

"One never feels really alive except on board ship," he said to me. "What do you think, M. Paoli?"

"I think, Sir," I replied, "that I must ask Your Royal Highness to allow me to differ. When I am on board ship, I sometimes feel more like dying."

"You're not the only one," he retorted, with a side glance at one of his equerries, who stood without wincing.

The prince liked teasing people; but his chaff was never cruel and he accompanied it with so much kindness that there was no question of taking offence at it. At heart, the prince had remained the middie that he once was, a "good sort," full of fun, full of "go," fond of laughing and interested in everything.

We chatted in the train until very late at night, for I did not leave the prince until we reached Modane, the station on the Italian frontier where my service ended.

2.

I saw him next at the Queen of Spain's wedding; and again in 1908. The prince and princess had just spent a week in Paris for the first time in their lives, and were returning to England delighted with their stay. The special train had hardly left the Gare du Nord, when the Hon. Derek Keppel, who was with the prince, came to me in my compartment:

"M. Paoli," he said, "I am commanded by Their Royal Highnesses to ask you to give them the pleasure of your company to luncheon."

I at once went to the royal saloon. The prince was chatting with M. Hua, his sons' French tutor, a very agreeable and scholarly man whom he treated as a friend; the princess was talking to Lady Eva Dugdale, her lady-in-waiting. It goes without saying that the conversation was all about Paris and the impressions which the prince and princess had received from their trips to Versailles, Chantilly, Fontainebleau and Chartres.

"I can understand my father's admiration and affection for France," said the prince to me. "It is a magnificent country and an interesting people. I am glad that the *entente cordiale* has strengthened the bonds of friendship between the two nations. I must come and see you oftener."

While the prince was saying these pleasant things to me, I was surprised to observe his valet depositing two apparently very heavy hampers on the floor in the middle of the carriage; but my astonishment was still greater when I saw the princess herself open one of the hampers and take out a table-cloth, plates, a chicken, tumblers, in short, a complete lunch.

"By the way," said the prince, "I forgot to tell you: there's no restaurant-car in the train, so we are going to have a pic-nic lunch here. It will be much better fun!"

And it was. The man put out two folding-tables which were in the carriage; and then, at the princess's suggestion, we all helped to lay the cloth! One looked after the plates, another the glasses, a third the knives and forks, while the princess herself carved the cold fowl.

When everything was at last ready, we sat down around this makeshift luncheon-table and, with a splendid will, did justice to our meal, which, I may say, was excellent. The proprietor of the Hôtel Bristol, who had undertaken to pack the hampers, had had the happy thought of adding a couple of bottles of champagne; and these were the cause of an incident that crowned the gaiety of this merry lunch. The prince declared that he would open them himself. Asking for the first bottle, he prepared to draw the cork with a thousand cunning precautions; but he certainly failed to reckon with the extraordinary impatience of that accursed cork, which was no sooner freed of its restraining bonds than it escaped from the prince's hands and went off like a pistol-shot, while the wine drenched the princess's dress. The prince was very sorry, but the princess laughed the thing off and declared that "it didn't stain." She had her skirt wiped down at once with water; and the luncheon finished as gaily as it began.

I could not give a more striking instance than the story which I have just told of the charming simplicity of this princess, in whom all the domestic virtues are so prettily personified. As I was taking leave of her on board the ship that was to convey the illustrious travellers from Calais to Dover:

"Do come and see us in England," she said. "I should like to show you my children: you have never met them."

"Madam," I replied, "I would do so with pleasure, if my duties allowed me to take a holiday. Meanwhile, may I respectfully remind Your Royal Highness that, on the last journey, you promised me the young princes' photograph?"

"That's true," she answered, "I forgot all about it. But, this time, wait." And, taking her handkerchief from her waistband, the princess made a knot in it. "Now I'm sure to remember," she added with a smile.

And, two days later, I received a splendid photograph of the children, adorned with their mother's signature.

Nearly three years have passed since this last journey and I have not had the honour of seeing King George and Queen Mary since. Nevertheless, they are good enough to think of me sometimes, as will be seen by the following affectionate letter which my friend Sir Arthur Bigge sent me on my retirement:

"MARLBOROUGH HOUSE,

"PALL MALL, S. W.

"Feb'y 28th, 1909.

"*My Dear Paoli,*—

"Your letter to me of the 24th inst. has been laid before the Prince and Princess of Wales, who received with feelings of deep regret the announcement that you had asked for and obtained permission to retire. Their Royal Highnesses are indeed sorry to think that they will never again have the advantage of your valuable services so efficiently and faithfully rendered and which always greatly conduced to the pleasure and comfort of Their Royal Highnesses' stay in France. At the same time the Prince and Princess rejoice to know that you will now enjoy a well-merited repose after 42 years of an anxious and strenuous service, and they trust that you may live to enjoy many years of health and happiness.

"Their Royal Highnesses are greatly touched by your words of loyal devotion and thank you heartily for these kind sentiments.

"As to myself, the thought of your retirement reminds me that a precious link with the past and especially with the memory of your great and beloved

Queen Victoria is now broken. I remember so well the first time we met at Modane when Her Majesty was travelling to Italy and you will ever be inseparably connected in my thoughts with those happy days spent in Her Majesty's service in France. I can well imagine what interest you will find in writing your book of reminiscences.

"Good-bye, my dear Paoli, and believe me to be

"Your old and devoted friend,

"ARTHUR BIGGE."

3.

I intended, in this chapter, to speak of those members of the royal family with whom my long and frequent service about the person of Queen Victoria gave me the occasion to come into contact; and I must not omit to mention a princess now no more, a woman of lofty intelligence and great heart, whom life did not spare the most cruel sorrows after granting her the proudest destinies. I refer to the Empress Frederick of Germany, eldest daughter of Queen Victoria and mother of William II.

I made her acquaintance in rather curious circumstances. It was at the naval review held by Queen Victoria in 1897, on the occasion of her diamond jubilee. As a special favour I was invited to see this magnificent sight on board the *Alberta* and I was gazing with wondering eyes at the majestic fleet of iron-clads through which the royal yacht had just begun to steam, when I heard a voice behind me say, in the purest Tuscan:

"*Bongiorno, Signor Paoli ...*"

I turned round. A woman, still young in bearing, though her face was crowned with grey hair under a widow's bonnet, stood before me with outstretched hand:

"I see," she said, smiling at my surprise, "that you do not know me. I am the Empress Frederick. I have often heard of you and I wanted to know you and to thank you for your attentions to my mother."

I bowed low, thinking what an uncommon occurrence it must be for a Frenchman to meet a German empress, talking Italian, on an English boat; and she continued:

"I know that you are a Corsican; and that is why I am speaking to you in your native language, which I learnt at Florence and which I love as much as I do my own."

The Empress Frederick, in fact, was remarkably well-educated, as are all the English princesses. She knew French as fluently as Italian and hardly ever spoke German, except to the chamberlain, Count Wedel. I was able to see, during our conversation, that she took a lively interest in my country; she asked me a thousand questions about France and particularly about French artists:

"I am a great admirer of M. Detaille's works," she said and added, after a pause, "He is very like the Emperor, my son. Don't you think so?"

I thought it the moment for prudence:

"I have never had the honour of seeing the Emperor William," I replied, "and therefore I cannot tell Your Imperial Majesty if the resemblance has struck me."

She then changed the conversation and spoke of the celebrations which were being prepared in her mother's honour.

The only other occasion on which I saw her was two years later, when she crossed French soil to go from England to Italy. This time, she was nervous and ill at ease:

"Do you assure me," she asked, as she landed at Calais, "that I shall meet with no unpleasantness between this and the Italian frontier?"

"Why, what are you afraid of, Ma'am?" I asked.

"You forget, M. Paoli, that I am the widow of the German Emperor and that, as such, I am no favourite in this country. Suppose I were recognised! There are memories, as you know, which French patriotism refuses to dismiss."

She was alluding not only to the events of 1870, but to the bad impression made in Paris by the visit which she had paid, a few years earlier—without any ulterior motive—to the ruined palace of Saint-Cloud, forgetting that it was destroyed and sacked by the Prussians. I reassured her, nevertheless, and said that I was prepared to vouch for the respect that would be shown her.

The journey, I need hardly say, passed off without a hitch. The Empress, with her suite, entered the private saloon-carriage of her brother, the Prince of Wales, which was coupled to the Paris mail-train and afterwards transferred to the Nice express, for the Empress was travelling to Bordighera, on the Italian Riviera.

She dared not leave her carriage during the short stop which was made in Paris; but, when we arrived at Marseilles the next morning, she said:

"I should awfully like to take a little exercise. I have been eighteen hours in this carriage!"

"But please do, Ma'am," I at once replied. "I promise you that nothing disagreeable will happen to you."

She thereupon decided to take my advice. She stepped down on the platform and walked about among the passengers. She was received on every side with marks of deferential respect—for, of course, her *incognito* had been betrayed, as every *incognito* should be—and suddenly felt encouraged to such an extent that, from that moment, she alighted at every stop. Gradually, indeed, as her confidence increased, she took longer and longer in returning to her carriage, so much so that she very nearly lost the train at Nice; and, when I took leave of her at Bordighera, she said, as she gave me her hand to kiss:

"Forgive me, my fears were absurd. Now, I have but one wish, to make a fresh stay in France. Who knows? Perhaps next year."

I do not know what circumstances prevented her from fulfilling her hopes; and the next time I heard of her was at Queen Victoria's funeral. I was astonished not to see her there and asked the reason of her chamberlain, Count Wedel, who sat beside me in St. George's Chapel at Windsor.

"Alas," he said, "our poor Empress is confined to her bed by a terrible illness! Think how she must suffer: her body is nothing but a living sore!"

A few months later, she was dead.

4.

I had only a more or less fleeting vision of this amiable sovereign, whose fate, though not so tragic as that of the Empress Elizabeth of Austria, was but little happier. On the other hand, I had opportunities of coming into much more frequent and constant contact with two of her sisters, Princess Christian of Schleswig-Holstein and Princess Henry of Battenberg.

Closely though these two princesses resemble each other in the admirable filial affection which they showed their mother, they are entirely different in disposition. Whereas the elder, who is generally known as the Princess Christian, is always ready to talk to those about her, Princess Beatrice, the younger, is comparatively silent and almost self-contained, but without the least affectation on her part: in fact, I have seldom met a princess more simple in her habits or more easy of access to poor folk. This contrast in their attitude towards life comes, I think, from a difference in their temperaments and tastes. The Princess Christian has inherited the homely virtues of the German princesses: she interests herself mainly in philanthropic and social questions. The Princess Henry, on the contrary, feels a marked attraction for literature and the arts, which she cultivates with a real talent; and, like all those who are endowed with an active brain, she loves to isolate herself from the outside world.

I must say that I never knew the Princess Christian as well as I did her sister, for the very good reason that she did not accompany Queen Victoria to France as often as the Princess Henry. Her arrival at Nice was usually later than that of the Queen and she very seldom remained until the end of Her Majesty's stay.

I remember, however, that, one year, they returned to England together; and, in this connexion, I can tell a story which goes to show how keenly alive the great of this earth can sometimes be to the smallest attentions paid them. The royal train, which had left Nice in the morning, pulled up, at five o'clock in the afternoon, as usual, at a little country station between Avignon and Tarascon, in order to enable the Queen to take her tea without being inconvenienced by the jolting of the wheels. Seeing me pacing the platform, the Princess Christian stepped out and walked up and down beside me. In the course of our conversation, she began to talk about her children:

"When I think," she said, with a certain melancholy, "that my daughter Victoria will be thirty years old to-morrow—for to-morrow is her birthday! How time flies!"

Princess Victoria was also one of the travelling-party. As soon, therefore, as the Princess Christian had left me, I scribbled a telegram to the special commissary at Caen, in Normandy, where we were to stop for a few minutes, on the following day, on our way to Cherbourg, and told him to order a bouquet and hand it to me as the train passed through.

The next morning, when we entered the station at Caen, I found my bouquet awaiting me: a modest spray consisting of all the rustic flowers of the fields which my worthy commissary had had gathered in the morning dew. I at once presented it to Princess Victoria, wishing her many happy returns of her birthday; and I cannot say which of the four of us—the Queen, the two princesses or I—was most touched by the loving gratitude which they all three expressed to me.

KING EDWARD ARRIVING AT THE ÉLYSÉE PALACE

KING EDWARD ON THE WAY TO CHURCH

5.

But, as I have said above, of all Queen Victoria's daughters, the one whom I knew best was the Princess Henry of Battenberg. In point of fact, she hardly ever left her august mother's side from the day when her married bliss received so cruel a blow in the tragic death of her husband and when the distress of mind found a refuge and peace in the affection of that same mother, whose heart was always filled with the most delicate compassion for every sorrow.

A close link had been formed between those two women: the Princess Henry had become the confidant of Queen Victoria's thoughts and was also, very often, the intermediary of her acts of discreet munificence. At Nice, she occupied the magnificent Villa Liserb, close to the hotel at which the Queen resided. Here I watched the games and the physical development of the princess's four children, Prince Alexander, Prince Maurice, Prince Leopold and little Princess Ena, little thinking that I should live to see the heavy crown of Charles V and Philip II placed upon the pretty, golden hair which was then still done up with pale-blue ribbons. Day after day, for many years, I saw those same children hail their grandmother's appearance with cries of delight.

The daily drive in the grounds of the Villa Liserb was in fact, one of Queen Victoria's favourite pleasures. She went there in her chair drawn by Jacquot, the white donkey, solemnly led by the Hindoo servant whose gaudy attire, like a monstrous flower, struck a loud note of colour against the green of the surrounding foliage. Slowly and smoothly, with infinite care, the little carriage advanced along the garden-paths which the pines, eucalyptus and olive trees shaded with their luxurious tresses. The Queen, holding the reins for form's sake, would cast her eyes from side to side in search of her grandchildren, who were usually crouching in the flower-beds or hiding behind the trees, happy in constantly renewing the innocent conspiracy of a surprise—always the same—which they prepared for their grandmother and which consisted in suddenly bursting out around her.

Or else a shuttlecock of a hoop would stray between Jacquot's legs.

"Stop, Jacquot!" cried the children.

And Jacquot, best-tempered of donkeys, would stop all the more readily as he knew that his patience would be rewarded with a lump of sugar.

The Princess Henry of Battenberg spent long hours in this wonderful smiling oasis, dividing her time between the education of her children, which she supervised and directed in person, and her own intellectual pursuits, to which she devoted herself ardently. She used to draw and paint very prettily, at that time; and she never forgot to take her sketch-book with her when accompanying the Queen on her drives in the neighbourhood of Nice. She sat and sketched while tea was being prepared in some picturesque spot where the royal carriage regularly made a prolonged halt.

She was a first-rate musician, played the harmonium on Sundays in the chapel of the Hôtel Regina and often went into the Catholic churches during the services in order to listen to the sacred music, which she preferred above all others. In this way, she came to appreciate more particularly the talent of a young organist called Pons, now a distinguished composer, who, at that time, used to play the organ at the church of Notre Dame at Nice. This artist, who was a native of the south of France, possessed a remarkable gift of improvisation which amazed the princess so greatly that she was always speaking of it to the Queen:

"You really ought to hear him," she would say.

"But he can't bring his organ to the hotel!" the Queen replied, laughing.

"Why should you not go to his church? I assure you that you will not be sorry."

The Queen, who was easily persuaded by her daughter, ended by consenting to visit Notre Dame one afternoon, on condition that she should be alone there, with her suite, during the little recital which the organist was to give for her benefit. Princess Beatrice, who was delighted at attaining her object, plied me with instructions so that the Queen might have a genuine artistic surprise:

"Be sure and see that there is no one in the church," she said to me, "and tell M. Pons to surpass himself."

I went and called on the rector and the organist. The former very kindly promised to take all the necessary steps for his Church to be quite empty during Her Majesty's visit. As for M. Pons, the honour which the Queen was doing him almost turned his head a little. He saw himself the equal of Bach and would have accosted Mozart by his surname if he had met him in the street.

"The Queen will be satisfied, I promise you," he declared, in his southern sing-song.

Things passed very nearly as we hoped. At the hour agreed upon, the royal landau stopped before the door of the church; the Queen, accompanied by the princess and a few persons of her suite, including myself, entered the great nave, where only a few float-lights lit up golden stars in the spacious darkness. When the Queen was seated in the arm-chair which I had sent on beforehand, Pons began to shed torrents of harmony upon our heads from his organ-loft above.

Nothing would have disturbed our meditation, but for a cat, an enormous black cat, which, after prowling behind the pillars, suddenly came up to the royal chair unperceived and jumped most disrespectfully into Her Majesty's lap! Picture the excitement! We drove it away. It returned. We tried to drive it away again. But it was stubborn in its affections and returned once more. Thereupon the Queen, who was more surprised than annoyed, resigned herself and accepted the curious adventure. She stroked the animal and kept it with her until the end of the recital.

6.

When Princess Henry of Battenberg did not accompany her mother on her drives—which happened very rarely—she liked going to the Empress Eugénie, who treated her as a daughter and who, as everybody knows, was the godmother of Queen Victoria Eugénie of Spain. The princess would sometimes spend the whole afternoon at the villa of Napoleon III's widow; one year indeed, she and Princess Ena stayed there all through the winter. Now, on this occasion, I happened to find myself placed in a very delicate position.

What occurred was this: the princess sent word to me, one day, with the Empress's consent, inviting me to dinner at the Villa Cyrnos. I was at first a little perplexed. It seemed to me a rather ticklish matter, considering my official situation, to figure at the table of the ex-Empress of the French. On the other hand, to refuse the invitation seemed tantamount to insulting the daughter of the Queen of England, to whom I was accredited. At last, I resolved to swallow my scruples and accepted.

That evening, after dinner, when thanking the Empress for her kindness, I could not help saying:

"I suppose, Madame, that there are very few officials of the Republic who would have dared to sit down at Your Majesty's table."

"To be equally frank with you," the Empress at once replied, laughing, "I will ask you to believe, my dear M. Paoli, that there are also very few officials of the Republic whom I should have cared to see seated there like yourself!"

7.

I must not close the story of the periods which I spent with the royal family at Nice without recalling that, on some of those occasions, I also met the Marchioness of Lorne, now Duchess of Argyll, and the Duke of Connaught;

but, to tell the truth, I only caught glimpses of them, because of the shortness of their visits.

I can also only mention quite casually the name of Queen Alexandra, for the charming lady has never stayed in France for any length of time. With the exception of two visits of forty-eight hours each, with which she honoured Paris when she went to France with King Edward, she has confined herself to passing through our country on her way to Denmark or to join the royal yacht at Marseilles or Genoa. On each of the journeys during which I was attached to her person, she gave me every sign of that captivating and bewitching kindness of which she alone appears to possess the secret. I also remember perceiving, as do all those who approach her, the touching affection that unites her to her sister, the Dowager Empress of Russia. Each time that she left her at Calais, to go either to Copenhagen or to the south, while the Empress Marie Feodorovna was returning to St. Petersburg, she never failed to say to me, in a voice full of anxiety:

"M. Paoli, do take great care of my sister. Watch over her attentively. I shall not know a moment's peace until I hear that she has arrived at the end of her journey."

The years have passed and it is not without pride that I reflect upon the fact that I have known four generations of that glorious royal family of England!

But, alas, it makes me feel no younger!...

X

THE KING OF CAMBODIA AND HIS DANCING-GIRLS

THE KING OF CAMBODIA

1.

I propose to conclude this stroll through my royal portrait-gallery with the entertaining story of the King of Cambodia. He was, so to speak, my last "client," at least the last of those whom I was "protecting" for the first time, for he had never set foot in France when, three years ago, I beheld him, in the bright light of a fine morning in June, greeting with a loud laugh the port of Marseilles, the gold-laced officials who had come to receive him, the soldiers, the sailors, the porters and the regimental band.

For he loved laughing. Hilarity with him was a habit, a necessity; it burst forth like a flourish of trumpets, it went off like a rocket at anything or nothing, suddenly lighting up his elderly monkey-face and revealing amidst the dark smudge that formed his features a dazzling key-board of ivory teeth.

Sisowath, King of Cambodia, struck me as a little yellow, dry, sinewy man who had been snowed upon, for amid his hard stubble of shiny black hairs there gleamed, over the temples, patches of white bristles that bore witness to his five and sixty summers. He still looked young, because of the slightness of his figure; and his costume consisted of a singular miscellany of Cambodian and European garments.

From the knees to the waist, his dress suggested the East. Starting from the frontier formed by his belt, the West resumed its rights and set the fashion of the day before yesterday! His feet were clad in shoes resembling a bishop's, with broad, flat buckles, whence rose two spindle-shanks confined in black silk stockings and ending in a queer pair of breeches of a thin, silky, copper-coloured material, something midway between a cyclist's knickerbockers and a woman's petticoat and known as the *sampot*, the national dress of Cambodia. Over these breeches of uncertain cut fell the graceless tails of an eighteenth-century dress-coat, opening over a shirt-front crossed by the broad ribbon of the Legion of Honour. Lastly, this astonishing get-up was topped with a rusty tall hat, dating back to the year 1830, which crowned the monarch's head.

All this made him look like a carnival-reveller who had come fresh from a fancy-dress ball. Nevertheless, he took himself very seriously; and the French government treated him with every consideration, for he represented a valuable asset in the exercise of our protectorate over Cambodia.

Those acquainted with the traditions of the Cambodian court will know that, in consenting to leave his realms for a time in order to go to France, he had broken every religious and political law. To appease the just wrath of Buddha and relieve his own conscience, before leaving his capital, Pnom-Penh, he had sent magnificent offerings to the tombs of the KneKne kings, bathed in lustral water prepared by the prayers of sixty-seven bonzes, invoked the emerald statue of the god Berdika and accepted at the hands of the chief Brahmin a leaf of scented amber, by way of a lucky charm.

It was really impossible to surround himself with more potent safeguards and he had every reason to be in a good humour, although he had flown into a great rage on the passage at seeing his suite abandoning themselves to the tortures of sea-sickness:

"I forbid you to be sick!" he shouted to them. "Those are my orders: am I the King or am I not?"

Distracted by the impossibility of obeying, they took refuge in the depths of the steamer and did not reappear on deck until the ship approached the Straits of Messina. And the saddened sovereign was made to realise for the first time that he was not omnipotent. The fact made so great an impression on his mind that, from that time forward, he became excessively and almost inconveniently polite. He shook hands with everybody he saw, beginning with the flunkeys at the Marseilles Prefecture, who lined the staircase as he went upstairs.

2.

Keen as was the interest taken by the public in Sisowath, it paled before the curiosity aroused by his dancing-girls. They formed an integral part of that extraordinary royal suite, in which figured three of his ministers, four of his sons, his daughter, two sons of King Norodom, his predecessor, and eleven favourites accompanied by a swarm of chamberlains, ladies of the bed-chamber and pages: women old and young, at whose breasts hung hideous little stunted, yellow, shrieking imps, from whom they had refused to be separated.

On the other hand, amid the disorder of that oriental horde, the *corps de ballet* constituted a caste apart, haughty, sacerdotal and self-contained. The twenty dancers came to France preceded by a great reputation for beauty. It may have been the result of beholding them in a different setting, under a different sky; but this much is certain, that they did not appear to me in the same light in which they had been depicted to us by enthusiastic travellers.

Sisowath's dancing-girls are not exactly pretty, judged by our own standard of feminine beauty. With their hard and close-cropped hair, their figures like those of striplings, their thin, muscular legs like those of young boys, their arms and hands like those of little girls, they seem to belong to no definite sex. They have something of the child about them, something of the young warrior of antiquity and something of the woman. Their usual dress, which is half feminine and half masculine, consisting of the famous *sampot* worn in creases between their knees and their hips and of a silk shawl confining their shoulders, crossed over the bust and knotted at the loins, tends to heighten this curious impression. But in the absence of beauty, they possess grace, a supple, captivating, royal grace, which is present in their every attitude and gesture; they have a perfume of fabled legend to accompany them, the sacred character of their functions to ennoble them; lastly, they have their dances full of mystery and majesty and art, their dances which have been handed down faithfully in the course of the ages and whose every movement, whose every deft curve remains inscribed on the bas-reliefs of the ruins of Ankor. For these reasons, they are beautiful, with the special beauty that clings to remote, inscrutable and fragile things.

They are all girls of good extraction, for it is an honour much sought after by the noble families of Cambodia to have a child admitted to the King's troop of dancers. Contrary to what has sometimes been asserted, the dancing-girls do not form part of the royal harem; they are considered a sort of vestals; virginal and radiant, they perform, in dancing, a more or less religious rite; and this is the only pleasure which they provide for their sovereign lord the King.

When they accompanied Sisowath to France, they were under the management of the King's own eldest daughter, the Princess Soumphady, an ugly, cross-grained old maid who ruled them with an iron hand. The "stars" were four principal dancers whose names seemed to have been picked, like the King's leaves of scented amber, in some sacred grove of Buddha's mysterious realm: they were called Mesdemoiselles Mih, Pho, Nuy and Pruong.

3.

When the whole party were landed, they had to be put up; and this was no easy matter. The Marseilles Prefecture was hardly large enough to house the King's fabulous and cumbrous retinue. We distributed its members over some of the neighbouring houses; but they spent their days at the Prefecture, which was then and there transformed into the camp of an Asiatic caravan. The ante-rooms and passages were blocked with pieces of luggage each quainter than the other. Heaped up promiscuously were jewel-cases, dress-trunks, cases of opium, bales of rice and sacks of coal, for the Cambodians, fearing lest they should fail to find in Europe the coal which they use to cook their rice, had insisted, at all costs, on bringing with them two-hundred sacks, which now lay trailing about upon the Smyrna rugs!

When, on the evening of his arrival, I pushed my way through this medley of incongruous baggage, to present myself to the King, of whom I had caught but a passing glimpse on the Marseilles quays, M. Gautret, the colonial administrator who had travelled with our guests, said to me:

"His Majesty is at dinner, but wishes to see you. Come this way."

Shall I ever forget that audience? Sisowath sat at a large table, surrounded by his family, his ministers, his favourites and his dancing-girls, while, squatting in a corner on the floor, were half-a-dozen musicians—His Majesty's private band—scraping away like mad on frail-sounding instruments. The King was eating salt-fish which had been prepared for him by his own cooks. He was the only one to use a knife and fork. The others did not care for such luxuries; at intervals, a waiter handed round a large gold bowl filled with rice, into which ministers, favourites, and dancing-girls dipped their hands, subsequently transferring the contents to their mouths.

When M. Gautret had mentioned my name and explained the nature of my functions, the King, who was gloating over his loathsome fish, looked up, gave me his hand and, with his everlasting noisy laugh, flung me a few vapid monosyllables:

"Glad ... Friend ... Long live France!"

Our conversation went on no further on that day. The next morning, we visited together the sights of Marseilles and its Colonial Exhibition. Sisowath, though very loquacious, was astonished at nothing, or at least pretended not to be. His dancers and favourites, on the other hand, were astonished at everything. They pawed the red-silk chairs for ever so long before venturing to sit upon the extreme edge, so great was their fear of spoiling them: most often, after a preliminary hesitation, they would end by settling down upon the floor, where they felt more at home. And yet they were not devoid of tact, as they showed when I took them, at the King's wish, to see the fine church of Notre Dame de la Garde, which, from the top of its rock, commands a view of the city, the surrounding country and the sea. They wanted to go up to the sanctuary and entered it with the same respectful demeanour which they would have displayed in the most sacred of their own pagodas. When we explained to them that the thousands of ex-votos which adorn the walls of the chapel represent so many tokens of pious gratitude, their eyes, like the King of Thule's, filled with tears and they suddenly prostrated themselves just as they might have done before the images of their own Buddhas.

During this time, the King, who had fished out a pair of white gloves and a white tie and adorned his *sampot* with an emerald belt, stood smiling at the Marseillaise, which was being performed in his honour, and, as I afterwards heard, smiling at the fair *Marseillese* as well.

Until then, I had enjoyed but a foretaste of the life and manners of the Cambodian Court. The stay which Sisowath and his suite were about to make in Paris was to enlighten me on this subject for good and all.

After three days' driving through the streets of Marseilles, the royal caravan set out for the capital, where the French government had resolved to give it an official reception and to entertain it at the expense of the nation. With this object in view, the government had hired a private house in the Avenue Malakoff and prudently furnished it from the national depository with chairs and tables "that need fear no damage."

Meanwhile, the Colonial Office had appointed me superintendent-in-chief of this novel "palace" and I had to take up my abode there during the whole of our royal guest's stay. The result was that, during the three weeks which I spent amid these picturesque surroundings, I enjoyed all the attractions of the most curiously exotic life that could possibly be imagined.

The bed-room allotted to me opened upon the passage containing the King's apartments; so that I may be said to have occupied a front seat at the permanent and delicious entertainment provided by the Cambodian court for the benefit of those admitted to its privacy.

What struck me first of all was the indiscreet familiarity of His Majesty's family and favourites. Princes, ministers and favourites, spent their lives in the passages and walked in and out of my room with an astonishing absence of constraint and in the airiest of costumes. If I happened to be at home, they paid no attention to my presence: they explored the room, poked about in the corners, tried the springs of my bed, asked me for cigarettes, examined my brushes and combs, smiled and went away. When I was out, they entered just the same, emptied my cigar and cigarette-boxes, sat down on my carpet and exchanged remarks that may have been jocular for all I know: I never found out.

Anxious to avoid any sort of friction, I made no complaint. I contented myself with locking up my personal belongings and replacing my boxes of Havanas with boxes of penny cigars; but my plunderers held different views; the ladies, especially, who had learnt to distinguish between good cigars and common "*Sénateurs*" expressed their rage and vexation with violent gestures and resolved thenceforth to give me the cold shoulder—which was more than I had hoped for.

There remained another drawback to which I had, willy-nilly to submit until the end. It consisted of Sisowath's unpleasant habit of walking up and down the passages at night, talking and laughing with his suite, while his orchestra tinkled out the "national" airs to an accompaniment of tambourines and cymbals and while the brats kept crying and squalling, notwithstanding the efforts of their mothers, who put lighted cigarettes between the children's lips to make them stop. It was simply maddening; and, when I tried to make a discreet protest, I was told that, as His Majesty took a siesta during the day, he had no need for sleep at night. The argument admitted of no reply and I had to accept the inevitable.

On the other hand, I enjoyed a few compensations. I was invited, from time to time, to assist at the King's toilet when he donned his gala clothes to go to an official dinner or a ceremony of one kind or another. After he had finished his ablutions—for he was always very particular about his person—his wives proceeded to dress him. They helped him into a gorgeous green and gold *sampot* and a brocaded tunic and put round his throat a sort of necklace resembling the gorget of a coat of mail and made of dull gold set with precious stones, ending at the shoulders in two sheets of gold that stuck out on either side like wings. They next girt his waist, arms and ankles with a belt and bracelets encrusted with exquisite gems. Lastly, they took away his rusty and antiquated old "topper" and gave him in exchange a wide Cambodian felt hat, surmounted by a kind of three-storied tower running into a point, adorned with gold chasings and literally paved with diamonds and emeralds. Thus attired, Sisowath looked very grand: he resembled the statue of a Hindoo god removed from its pagoda.

Nevertheless, western civilisation began stealthily to exert its formidable influence over his tastes, if not his habits. We had not been a week in Paris before our guest thought it better, on his afternoon excursions, to replace the *sampot* with the conventional European trousers and his out-of-date cutaway with a faultless frock-coat. But for his yellow complexion, his slanting eyes and his woolly hair, he would have looked a regular dandy!

Ever eager to appear good-natured and polite, he kissed the daughters of the hall-porter at the Colonial Office, each time he went to the Pavillion de Flore, and shook hands with the messengers at the Foreign Office and with all the salesmen at the Bon Marché, which he made a point of visiting. Again, when passing through the Place Victor-Hugo, he never failed to take off his hat with a great flourish to our national poet. Lastly, I had the greatest difficulty in keeping him from sending sacred offerings to the tomb of Napoleon I, "whom we hold in veneration in Cambodia," he explained to me through the interpreter. Hearing, on the other hand, that European sovereigns are accustomed to leave their cards on certain official personages, he asked me to order him a hundred worded as follows:

PREAS BAT SOMDACH PREAS SISOWATH
CHOM CHAKREPONGS.

4.

Nevertheless, in spite of the ever fresh surprises which Paris had in store for him and of their undoubted attraction for his mind, the King soon began to feel a certain lassitude:

"Paris," he said to me, "is a wonderful, but tiring city. The houses are too high and there are too many carriages. How is it that you still allow horse-carriages? If I were the master here, I would abolish them and allow nothing but motors."

When he had visited the public buildings and done the sights and been to Fontainebleau and Versailles and Compiègne and had the mechanism of the phonographs and cinematographs explained to him he began to bore himself. He then thought of his dancing-girls, whom he had left behind at Marseilles, and sent for them to Paris on the pretext of exhibiting them at a garden-party given by the president of the republic at the Élysée. One fine morning, they all landed at the Gare de Lyon, a little bewildered, a little flurried, in the charge of the grim Princess Soumphady, who was dressed in a violet *sampot*, with a stream of diamonds round her neck. They arrived looking like so many lost sheep, accompanied by their six readers, their eight singers, their four dressers, their two comedians and their six musicians.

The dancers' advent created quite a sensation in the district of the Avenue Malakoff. They were quartered opposite the royal "palace," in a building at the back of a courtyard, and, when at last good King Sisowath saw them from his balcony, a broad smile of happiness lit up his yellow face.

They rehearsed their ballets every morning in a large room that did duty as a theatre. I was allowed to look on, as a special favour, and I was thus able to watch pretty closely those curious and amazingly artistic little creatures and their dances.

Their ballets always began with a musical prelude performed upon brass and bamboo instruments. Then, while some of the women struck up a religious chant and others clapped their hands in measured time, the dancers left the group one by one, shooting out and meeting in the ring; and a regular fanciful, childish drama was suggested by their movements, their gestures and their attitudes, which contrasted strangely with the sacerdotal repose of their features. They looked, at one time, like large, living flowers; at another, like automatic dolls.

The dances provided an odd medley of Moorish and Spanish steps. Sometimes, the stomach would sway to and fro, as though one were watching a dance of Egyptian almes; at other times, the legs quivered and the dancer stamped her feet, raised her arms, jerked her hips as though she meant to give us some Andalusian *jota* or *habanera*. And in those faces, which seemed inanimate beneath their fixed smiles, nothing allowed the inner feelings of the soul to penetrate: yet what suggestive mimicry was there, what harmonious poses and what marvellous costumes!

The Cambodian ballet-girls, when dancing in public, wear clothes that are simply fairy-like. They have bodices of silk stitched with gold and adorned with precious stones. These bodices are very heavy and are fitted upon them and sewn before each performance, so they form as it were a new skin and reveal with a clearness that is nothing short of impressive the slightest undulations of the body.

The dressers take two or three hours to clothe the dancers, after which they paint the girls' faces and deck them out with bracelets, necklaces and rings of priceless value. Sometimes also the dancers' fingers are slipped into long, bent, golden claws, which describe harmonious curves in space.

Lastly, the head-dress consists of either the traditional *pnom*—a sort of pointed hat, all of gold and fastened on by clutches that grip the head—or a wreath of enormous flowers, or else of a pale-tinted silk handkerchief rolled low over the temples.

**KING SISOWATH'S DANCERS BEFORE THE PRESIDENT
AT THE ÉLYSÉE PALACE**

The dancers and their dances achieved, as may be imagined, no small success, first at the Elysée and afterwards in the Bois de Boulogne, where a gala performance was given, in the open-air theatre of the Pré Catelan, by the light of the electric lamps. Between whiles, they took drives through Paris, which gave rise to all sorts of astonished and enthusiastic manifestations on their part, much to the delight of their guides; for they had the mental attitude of little girls and, when, after a week, they had to go back to Marseilles, where they formed the principal attraction at the Colonial Exhibition, their despair was something immense. It was as much as we could do to console them by presenting them all with mechanical rabbits and unbreakable dolls.

And the King, once more, was bored. He was so thoroughly bored that, a few days after the departure of his ballet-girls, he resolved to go and spend a couple of days at Nancy, in order to see a dozen or two young Cambodians who had been attending the local industrial school for the last twelve-month. The organising of this visit was very troublesome, for the King had acquired a taste for military display and insisted upon being received at Nancy with full honours, such as he had been used to in Paris. Worse still, the trip very nearly ended in disaster, entirely through Sisowath's own fault.

The inhabitants of Nancy, amused and delighted by the show of Oriental luxury that met their eyes, gave the King an enthusiastic ovation far in excess of his expectations. His gratitude was such that, on the evening of his arrival, he took it into his head to manifest his delight by flinging handfuls of silver through the windows of the Prefecture to the crowd that stood cheering him on the Place Stanislas! The reader can picture the effect of this beneficent shower. Suddenly, loud cries and shouts were heard and a regular battle was fought in front of the Prefecture, for one and all wished to profit by the royal largesse.

I at once rushed up to the King and begged him to stop this dangerous game. But Sisowath, who was madly diverted by the sight, positively refused to yield to my entreaties. He even asked to have a thousand-franc note changed for gold.

Seeing that persuasion was of no avail, I took a quick and bold resolve. I had him removed from the window by force, undeterred by the insults with which he overwhelmed me in the Cambodian tongue.

But I had not yet come to the end of my emotions: a serio-comic incident followed apace. Sisowath, suddenly evading the watchfulness of my inspectors, who dared not detain him like a common malefactor, escaped, darted down the stairs, four steps at a time, opened a window on the ground floor and, with hoarse cries, began to fling into the square all the *louis d'or* which he had in his possession. The moment he heard us coming, quick as lightning he was off and flew to another window. For a quarter of an hour, a mad steeple-chase was kept up through all the rooms of the Prefecture, amid the roars of the excited crowd in the streets.

Fortunately, the King soon grew tired and accepted his defeat. As for me, I naturally looked upon my disgrace as assured. But Sisowath, thank goodness, was not vindictive. The next morning, he gave me his hand and, bursting into loud laughter, contented himself with saying:

"Very funny!"

5.

A week later, he took ship at Marseilles, with his court, to return to Cambodia. When I said good-bye to him on the deck of the steamer, he appeared heart-broken at having to leave our country. Heart-broken, too, seemed the little dancing-girls squatting at the foot of the mast, with their mechanical rabbits and their unbreakable dolls—the last keepsake to remind them of their stay in Paris—which they squeezed fondly in their arms.

When, at length, the hour of parting had struck, good King Sisowath, greatly moved, called me to his side:

"Here," he said. "Present for you."

And he handed me a parcel done up in a pink-silk handkerchief.

As soon as I was on shore, I hastened to open it; to my great confusion, it contained a splendid *sampot* made of fine cloth of gold. The King of Cambodia had presented me with his state breeches, which were all that remained to me of my last "client" and of my Oriental dreams!

FOOTNOTES:

[1] In France, the premiership is very often held in conjunction with the portfolio of the Interior, or Home Office.—*Translator's Note.*

[2] The *habit à la française*, once a military cloak, now used purely for livery, is a heavily embroidered coat, similar to that of an English flunkey, but of a less voluminous cut and shorter.—*Translator's Note.*

[3] "Oho! An empress comes this way!"—*Translator's Note.*

[4] *Jonkheer* is a Dutch hereditary title of nobility, ranking below that of baron.—*Translator's Note.*

[5] The family of Dumonceau is of Belgian origin and derives from an ancestor in the parish of Saint-Géry, Brussels.—*Translator's Note.*

[6] Boniface of Savoy was nominated to the Archbishopric of Canterbury, in 1241, by King Henry III of England, who had married Boniface's niece Eleanor, daughter of Raymond Berengar, Count of Provence, and Beatrix of Savoy.—*Translator's Note.*

[7] The late King of the Belgians shared the national peculiarity of interlarding his French with a succession of *savez-vous*.—*Translator's Note.*

Booksophile
Your Local Online Bookstore

Buy Books Online from
www.Booksophile.com

Explore our collection of books written in various languages and uncommon topics from different parts of the world, including history, art and culture, poems, autobiography and bibliographies, cooking, action & adventure, world war, fiction, science, and law.

Add to your bookshelf or gift to another lover of books - first editions of some of the most celebrated books ever published. From classic literature to bestsellers, you will find many first editions that were presumed to be out-of-print.

Free shipping globally for orders worth US$ 100.00.

Use code "Shop_10" to avail additional 10% on first order.

Visit today
www.booksophile.com

Milton Keynes UK
Ingram Content Group UK Ltd.
UKHW010827141223
434360UK00004B/313